Never Surrender!

A true story

Sonja, Amsterdam 1943

Seaside Press

Liliane Pelzman

Seaside Press, POB 5427 Santa Monica, CA 90409.
www.neversurrender.me
ISBN-13:   978-0-615-39626-2
ISBN-10:   0-615-39626-7

Front Cover poster: Beeldbank WO2 Nederlands Instituut voor
Oorlogsdocumentatie.
Printed in the United States of America
Fourth edition/f

Get it all on record now because somewhere down the road of history, some bastard will get up and say that this never happened.

-Dwight D. Eisenhower, five-star general, the United States Army and the 34th President of the United States

General Dwight D. Eisenhower visits the concentration camp at Ohrdruf with Generals Bradley and Patton

In memory of:

Henrietta & Jacob, Herman, Judie, uncle Maurits, aunt Wilhelmina grandmother Judickje, uncle Felix and uncle Jack, uncle Elie and aunt Jette, uncle Philip & aunt Clara, cousins Sara and Beppie cousins Aaron and Meijer, Irma, Betty, Jenny and many more

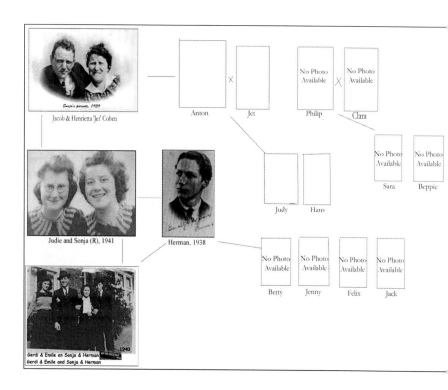

Acknowledgements

For my mother Sonja who survived with grace.

Without the love and support of my family and friends, I would not have finished this project. Without the feedback of the students, I would not have started it.

I'm especially grateful to:

Bram Benjamins and Dr. I. Berkovitz, my mentors on this path, Stephen Brown, Jennifer Cordey, Sima Har-Lev, Dennis and June Horner, Mischa Kiek, Robert Kiek, Mary Lynn Navarro, Connie Otten, Yaron Pelzman, Marianne van Praag, Mary and Robin Sheldon.

Foreword

In 1943 in Holland, on a cold February morning, Sonja and Herman Rosenstein, sweethearts since high school, twenty years old and newly married, boarded a train in Holland, bound for the town of Theresienstadt in Czechoslovakia.

They were madly in love. They knew no fear and no anxiety. They were full of hope and optimism and ready for an adventure. They thought they were going to work a few months. Instead, Herman was killed and Sonja came back from Auschwitz with a story. This is her story.

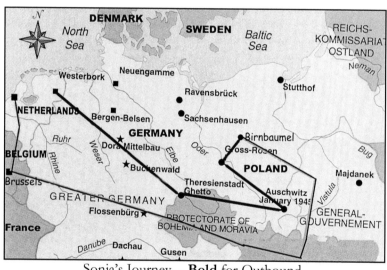

Sonja's Journey -- **Bold** for Outbound

***

Contents

1. Herman   10

2. Life seemed good   13

3. The Beginning   17

4. Safe for now   21

5. Lunch   25

6. Orders to report   28

7. Hiding   33

8. Problem solved   39

9. Herman arrested   44

10. Westerbork   47

11. The End of the Beginning   54

12. Theresienstadt   58

13. From Bad to Worse   65

14. Auschwitz - Birkenau   68

15. Skin and Bones   80

16. The Beginning of the End   87

17. Undetermined   91

18. Displaced Persons   95

19. Home   98

20. Young legs   100

21. Where is Herman?   102

22. Epilogue   109

23. Q & A   110

In April 1924, Hitler served nine months of a five-year prison term. While in prison, he started working on My Battle, in which he explained his plans for the Third Reich (Empire).

***

Amsterdam, Holland, 1943, June 20th. It was a warm Sunday morning. Holland had been occupied by Nazi Germany for three years now. At around ten-thirty, Sonja walked to work. Her mind was with her beloved and brand new husband Herman. It had been four longs weeks since his arrest and his deportation to Camp Westerbork. It was unbearable. When was she going to see him again?

All of a sudden, a car and a truck screamed into the street from opposite ends and came to a screeching halt. The sound of shrill whistles suddenly filled the peaceful street. About ten police officers with angry barking dogs jumped from the back of the truck and ran up to anybody wearing a yellow star. SS men motioned spectators to move on.

The driver of the truck saw Sonja's star on her coat. "Papers," he barked at her.

She handed him her ID.

"Come on, get in."

Terrified she climbed into the back of the truck. Men, women, and a few children sat packed side-by-side on facing benches. They made room for her. The driver dropped the canvas cover and climbed behind the wheel. She heard him say, "We've got enough of them for now." He was referring to the Jews quota for the day.

1. Herman

In the mid to late 1930s, many Jewish families fled from Germany to neighboring Holland. Their kids enrolled in Dutch schools.

*Holland/Netherlands and Germany

***

*Holland was the name of one of the original provinces. It stuck as a popular name and became a synecdoche for the Netherlands.

Herman Rosenstein went to school in Lübeck, Germany, where one day after his PE class, some friends teased him about being circumcised. Was he Jewish, they'd asked.

After school, he'd asked his mother about it.

"Because it's more hygienic," she had answered him.

Irma sat him down and told him about his biological father, a German soldier, a man she had loved very much and planned to marry. But their plans were thwarted and they were no longer allowed to be friends. As he told her about the name calling in school, his mom decided Germany had become too dangerous for her son. Her sister Betty lived in Amsterdam. Her son had recently married and moved out. Herman got his room.

Sonja and Herman met while walking to school. They became instant friends. She liked his accent. He was handsome. She definitely liked him. He liked her looks and her voice. He loved hearing her sing. She was exactly one day his junior.

Sonja usually left for school at twenty of nine, now she wanted to leave at eight. Her mother knew about Herman. She had met him and was not impressed.

"Finish your breakfast," her mom ordered sternly.

After school, they walked home together hand in hand; making sure her mother didn't not see them.

There was no Facebook or Twitter, there were no cell phones, it was just them, and they loved their uninterrupted quiet moments together.

It was a shame though, that she wasn't allowed to bring him home. Her girlfriends were, why wasn't she?

Then her parents relented.

"Where are you kids doing today?"

"Gerdi is playing a basket ball game today. We're going to watch."

"I want her home before dinner," her mom said strictly to Herman.

"Of course Ms. Cohen."

They knew that from behind the window, her mother kept watching until they turned the corner. As soon as they did, they stopped and kissed. They kissed whenever they could, and if they weren't kissing, they were holding hands. She liked that about him.

The city gave permission to run a German ex-pat club. The club sponsored cultural events, and offered history, art, and language classes. The camping trips were very popular. Herman played table tennis with his friends at the club every day and quickly became known as an ace player. On Sundays, members got together and coffee was served. Anne Frank's dad was a member there too.

In 1938, when Herman was sixteen years old, he switched to a technical college, where he studied automotive mechanics. This gave him a chance to study and make money at the same time. Soon after switching schools, the Committee for Jewish Refugees offered him a job. The CJR was the link between the Dutch government and the German refugees. CJR helped with immigration papers and assisted with housing, work permits, financial matters, and so forth.

In charge of the CJR was a lawyer from Vienna. He offered Herman a position as his assistant and Herman gratefully accepted. His German was fluent and they could use a bright guy like him. They celebrated his good fortune at the club.

"I wish my mother could see me now."

"What was she like? I want to meet her someday."

"You will. I'm making good money. I'll take you."

"One day."

2. Life seemed good

January 1933. Hysteria is sweeping Europe. Hitler became Reich's Chancellor of Germany. You were with him or not. Scores were settled. Opponents disappeared into concentration camp Dachau. The Nazi party flag, a black swastika on a red background, flew alongside Germany's national flag.

In 1934, as one of his first major foreign policy initiatives, Hitler signed a nonaggression pact with Poland.

In 1933, he organized a national boycott against Jewish businesses.

In 1937, Henry Ford received the Cross of the German Eagle Order from Hitler.

In 1938, the Dutch borders closed for refugees. Border guards were instructed to send them back to Nazi Germany. Back in Germany, the Gestapo, the Secret State Police, sent them to concentration camps.

Austrians welcomed Hitler with flowers. He was born there; he was one of their own. They were proud of him in 1938.

***

Jacob started his own business. Bolts of fabric, mostly silks and wool, were piled up in the spare bedroom. He liked having his own business and was confident about the future.

On Saturdays, Sonja, now fifteen years old, met up with her dad after service and they walked home together. She quietly sang an aria for him from some opera or other. Her dad glowed as he proudly noticed that his little girl was turning into a beautiful young woman.

In 1938, a few days before summer break started, Sonja fell during PE and badly hurt her knee. Uncle Anton, a medical doctor and her mom's brother, was her favorite uncle. He approved her going to Zandvoort as planned, if she promised not to move her leg a whole lot. On the beach, before leaving with her mom for lunch, her sister built a mound of sand for Sonja's knee to rest on.

She missed Herman terribly and as soon as her mom and sister left for lunch, she got a pen and paper out and wrote him a letter. Then she'd read from to a pile of books, while waiting for her mom and her sister to return with her lunchbox.

Halfway through their vacation, uncle Anton came all the way from Amsterdam to check up on her knee. She heard him tell her mom that he had treated German refugee that day, who'd been in a camp called Dachau. It sounded horrible. Apparently, many people died there. Anton commented, "If it's all true, we're in for something, but the stories are probably exaggerated."

"Take it easy on the walking and you'll be fine." Anton told Sonja before heading back to Amsterdam with Sonja's letters for Herman.

In Amsterdam, in the mean time, Herman like all refugees was required to report once a month to the police station where they renewed his residence permit. His papers were in order, he was making money, and he was in love with Sonja. Life seemed good.

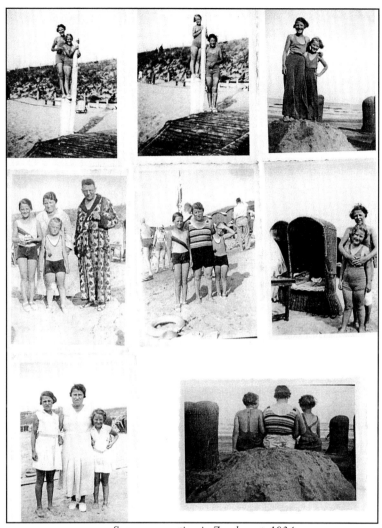

Summer vacation in Zandvoort, 1934

For the most part, the Dutch Jews disregarded the doomsday stories. It did not concern them. They were convinced those shocking things could never happen in Holland.

"This is Holland. Nothing can happen to us here."

A few months before the beginning of the war, Anton took his family on a short vacation to Paris. There were signs posted along the road that read: IF YOU ARE NOT FRENCH, YOU ARE AN ENEMY. Jet was worried.

"Anton, perhaps we should leave and take a boat to the United States. Let's not go back to Holland." But Anton did not want to abandon his patients. He offered to drive to Le Havre and put Jet and the children on a ship bound for the United States, but Jet did not want to leave without him.

Sonja loved opera. She knew many arias by heart. In 1938, her mom had Sonja's voice tested by Cato Engelen-Sewing, a well-known opera singer in those days. Cato recommended singing lessons. Cato's schedule was booked but she told them, if Sonja was willing to wait, they could come back a few months later. Herman was so proud of her.

3. The Beginning

May 10th, 1940. On a Friday morning at four o'clock, Nazi Germany invaded Holland, last occupied by Napoleon in 1815. By sunrise, seventy-four divisions of Hitler's army were raging through the Low Countries and Belgium. Holland succumbed mostly to Hitler's air force. Twin-engine Junkers JU-88 started bombing Amsterdam airport and other airfields, transport planes carried paratroopers. Above airfields, bridges, and other strategic points, the airplanes reduced speed to let paratroopers jump. Crates with weapons and munitions were thrown after them. By early afternoon, 1200 Luftwaffe troops were in charge of most of the airfields. To speed up Holland's surrender, Field Marshall Herman Göring had the city of Rotterdam bombed. When the Nazis threatened to bomb the city of Utrecht, the Dutch army surrendered. Capitulation papers were signed the following day.

Twin-engine Junkers JU-88

***

17

Daybreak on May 10th, 1940. The night had been unusually warm. The bedroom window was partly open. The monotonous drone of airplanes woke them up. Sonja and her sister went to the window. The sky was teeming with airplanes. Sonja was not sure what to think of it. Her finals worried her more than those airplanes. She was intent on graduating. She got dressed and read over her homework. With a little luck, she could sneak out and meet up with Herman before school.

Her parents now too were awake. The four watched in disbelief as they saw an endless stream of airplanes against the blue sky. The forecast for Friday was sunny and warm. Her father looked worried.

"The sun won't be shining for us today," her father had commented.

Sonja wanted to study nursing, but her mother advised her to get a secretarial diploma. She passed her finals and the secretary course and found a job as a secretary. Her boss was more interested in her than in her work. From time to time, he bought her a bottle of perfume. Her mother was skeptical, but didn't comment. She was proud of her daughter, who had insisted on pulling her weight and handed her two-thirds of her paycheck every month.

The first couple of weeks into the German invasion, nothing noticeably changed. Although they knew of the social and economic hardships in Nazi Germany, Dutch Jews were still convinced that such things could never happen in Holland.

But, things started changing slowly. Small groups of national socialists, mostly uneducated and unemployed thugs, started harassing Jews in movie theaters, stores, and restaurants. If someone looked Jewish, they walked up to them, picked a fight, and beat them to a pulp. Police officers turned a blind eye.

First, Jews were expelled from the Civil Defense Force. One of the responsibilities of the CDF was to make sure that curtains were properly closed to prevent enemy aircraft from finding their way. Showing light earned a steep fine. The next directive ordered Jewish butchers to close down.

Around Easter holiday, the tiny fishing village of Zandvoort became the first town in Holland that made renting rooms to Jews illegal. Zandvoort went into history as the first town to post signs reading, "NO JEWS ALLOWED."

Now that they couldn't go there on vacation any more, Jet surprised her daughters with brand new, dazzling-looking bicycles. They loved their spotless shiny bikes and their parents happily noticed their disappointment was quickly a thing of the past.

That first summer of the Nazi takeover, Sonja lived for the weekends and the picnic parties in the park. On Sundays, after cleaning her room, she prepared a picnic basket. She felt ecstatic because she knew that Herman was waiting for her. As soon as her mom had inspected her room, she kissed her and took off.

They rode their bikes to the park, where they met up with Gerdi and Emile and a group of his mostly German friends. Gerdi and Emile's parents had come from Poland, from a small-unknown town called Oswiecim, later known by its German name as Auschwitz. They had moved to Amsterdam where they expected to be safe, because Amsterdam had remained quiet during World War I (1914-1918).

After the usual joking and chitchatting, Herman played a game of soccer. His first goal was for her. After the game he dared her to swim with him to the island in the center of the lake, from where they'd look at the full moon rising. He'd tell her the difference between waxing and waning and about the blue moon. About the stars, the constellation, and the Big Dipper. She had laughed and asked him how he knew all that stuff. She'd loved it when he told her that by looking at the moon you connected with someone you loved. His mother had told him that when he'd left Germany. He looked up at the moon, and as if talking to his mom he told her she needn't worry. He was happy. He placed Sonja's hand on his heart. She adored him, and he her.

At the end of another great Sunday, they rode back together

and kissed before Sonja continued home alone with a big smile on her face, because he had just told her: "As long as I live, I will love you."

Also, she figured that it suited her just fine not going to Zandvoort anymore. Between the new bike and Herman, this summer had been pretty close to perfect, even with the Germans there.

For her eighteenth birthday, her parents gave her a typewriter. She was a good typist and took good shorthand. Her dad's business had grown. She was proud to help any way she could. She was close to both her parents, but her father was her absolute hero.

Ninotchka starring Greta Garbo and *First Love* starring Dianne Durbin played in the theaters.

It had become a tradition on Wednesdays, for her mom to take Sonja and her sister to the movies. The last movie they saw together was *The Great Waltz*, with Milizia Korjus. A week later, it had become illegal, according to the signs posted outside the theaters: No Jews Allowed.

4. Safe for now

Public places became off limits. Signs appeared in windows of hotels, cafés, restaurants, swimming pools, museums, libraries, parks, markets, anywhere public. Most of them still believed that if it wouldn't get any worse, they'd be able to handle it.

After Jewish Councils proved an efficient strategy in Poland, Germany, Austria, and Czechoslovakia, the Nazis established the Jewish Council (JC) in Holland. The JC were puppets or errand boys doing the Nazis' dirty work, such as registering the Jewish population throughout the country. They cooperated, hoping to save lives. Besides, if they refused, they were deportation. The JC's first task was to keep the Jews advised of the ever-increasing deluge of new directives. They were responsible for ensuring that the new rules that were published in the Jewish Weekly.

The Nazi government knew that people who had an exemption stamp felt safe and wouldn't hide. They let the JC issue exemption stamps to all their employees, in fact the JC issued as many stamps to as many people as it possible could justify. Family and friends, friends of friends, they were all issued stamps, supposedly working for the JC. Overall, the JC "employed" thousands of people. A stamp meant you were needed and that would postpone your deportation to Poland.

A new law was published ordering Jews to declare their assets. Soon after, their accounts were frozen and everybody Jewish was choked financially.
The JC received small amounts of money to be distributed amongst the members of their community. It was a shrewd application of the carrots and sticks tactic. Just as they felt hopeless, they received a check.

In the summer of 1942, the JC was ordered to draw up a list of persons who were to be sent "to work in the East." Following an intense internal debate, the council agreed to provide the Germans with 7,000 names. For this action and for other instances of compliance with German orders, the JC in Holland was severely criticized after the war was over 1945.

No Jews allowed 1942

***

Major Lages (pronounced Lahges) was the Nazi top man responsible for the fate of the Jews in Holland. His captain was in charge of operations, i.e. getting the Jews packed and ready, and on the train. The captain, Aus der Funten, was from Vienna, so was Herman's boss. They knew each other from school. They'd met on opposing debate teams. They were never friends, but they respected each other. The captain appointed Herman's boss as his point man for the day-to-day planning and supervision of the deportations. Herman's boss brought Herman in as his assistant.

Major Willy Lages

Lages reported to Eichman's office in Berlin. Berlin had complained that getting rid of the Jews in Holland was taking too long. The major told his captain and the captain told Herman's boss to speed it up.

The major and his captain differed in their approach and a period of infighting and backbiting started between them. They discredited each other in Berlin, and it was no secret that the major didn't care for anyone from the captain's team, which included Herman and his boss.

Herman was not interested in politics but suddenly he found himself in an authoritative position. A couple of times a day, he carried confidential paperwork from his boss to Aus der Fünten's office. Aus der Fünten liked him, "Are you sure you are Jewish?" Herman knew exactly why he'd asked. His mom had told him about Chaim Rosenstein not being his biological father. His father was a German soldier. Every time he'd wanted to tell Sonja, he'd changed his mind. He'd tell her after the war was over. For now, looking and sounding German worked to his advantage.

When he went to renew his December residence permit, they told him at the police station, that he did not need a permit anymore.

"You won't be needing your passport anymore either. I will keep that for you. Thank you very much."

"I have great news," he told Sonja later that day, "I'm allowed to stay indefinitely.

No need to worry anymore." They were relatively happy days.

When the war broke out, Sonja and her family lived on the top floor. They were safe for now, so they thought.

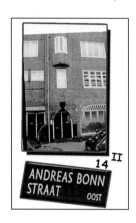

5. Lunch

The Wannsee Conference happened in January 1942. Hitler was getting rid of the Jews, but a bullet or two per person was too costly and too time consuming. The concentration camps were packed. There was a storage problem. On a winter day during an official lunch in the Berlin suburb of Wannsee, fifteen high-ranking Nazi officers tried to find a solution to the problem.

By the time the men were ready for dessert, their storage problem was solved. Working toward greater efficiency, they decided to replace manual executions with gas chambers. To shorten the walk to the gas chambers, they planned to extend railroad tracks right into the camps. That lunch affected the lives of every Jew in occupied Europe, including Sonja and Herman's and their families.

The infamous Wannsee villa where the lunch was held.

***

In 1942, when Herman returned home from work, his aunt Betty sat waiting for him in a dark living room.

"What's wrong?" He turned the light on. She motioned silently to a postcard on the table. He saw the Red Cross on the front of the card.

"Why would the Red Cross send me a card?"

He recognized his mother's handwriting. His mother and father, his sister and his newborn baby brother had moved to the ghetto of Lodz. Herman was not aware of the circumstances. He gazed at the card. He didn't understand.

"Perhaps," he said to his aunt, "they wanted to move to a bigger place?"

Betty got up quietly. She checked that the curtains were properly closed and went to the kitchen to prepare his dinner.

Sonja and Herman met at Gerdi's whenever they could get away. Then something happened they worried about. Sonja thought she was pregnant. They discussed their options. Getting married was out of the question. Her parents would never allow it. This was not a good time to have a baby. Pregnant women and mothers with babies were deported.

The downstairs neighbor had a three-year-old. Sonja wanted to ask her for advice. They had a cup of tea and Sonja looked at the wedding picture in the living room.

"That's the kind of dress I want to wear when Herman and I get married—with a beautiful, long, white veil."

"How is Herman?"

"He's fine. We're going to the theater this afternoon."

She changed her mind about asking advice. Back upstairs, she found her mother in her bedroom, with the contents of her purse scattered on her bed.

"What are those pills?" her mother yelled at the top of her lungs.

Sonja started to cry. "I am late."

Her mom called her dad. He came home and told her to stay in her room.

When Herman came to pick her up, her dad answered the door. From her bedroom, Sonja heard bits and pieces of their conversation.

"Hello. I am here to pick up Sonja. We are going to the theater," she heard him say politely.

"You're not going anywhere with my daughter, and you are not to see her again."

She'd never heard her father that angry. When she heard the front door close, she cried herself to sleep. When she woke up, she found she wasn't expecting after all, but all the same, she was never to see Herman again. The following day they met at Gerdi's.

It had taken Jacob five years to build a good-running business. The girls were healthy and happy. Sonja liked her job and her sister Judie was doing well in school.

Jacob had wanted to move to a bigger home, but his business had been confiscated and his plans had come to a sudden halt. With no income, and no access to money, he sold the last bit of fabric he had in stock. Was he still thinking that everything was going to be fine?

Every week, the *Jewish Weekly* published new regulations. When they were no longer allowed to drive, Anton parked his car at a friend's garage. When they were ordered to turn in their bikes, Sonja and Judie sadly surrendered them. Using public transport was against the law and sometimes Sonja walked thirty minutes to Gerdi's, where she met up with Herman for half an hour before she had to rush home.

One time she ran into a friend, who'd been lucky.

"Lucky how?" Sonja asked.

"I volunteered. They are sending me to Poland. I'm so excited. I've always wanted to travel."

She left for Auschwitz and three days later, she was dead.

6. Orders to report

In May, the Jewish Weekly announced that it was mandatory to sew a yellow Star of David onto three layers of clothing; overcoat, jacket and blouse. Instructions specified the exact location. If you didn't and were found out, you were immediately deported. They paid for their own stars. Some non-Jews pinned one on to show solidarity, but they were arrested.

The top Nazi brass in Berlin had decided that by December of 1942, 15,000 Dutch Jews must have been deported from Holland for Poland. Now Lages had a quota to fill or he'd be trouble with Berlin. Fifteen thousand Jews by the end of the year had to be deported. He told Aus der Fünten that mailing those notices wasn't fast enough.

He wanted them hand delivered. The police was working overtime. At first, they rang the bell, handed over the notices, and wished the person at the door good night. That also took too long. Bell ringing turned into door banging. If they didn't open fast enough, they kicked the door in and ordered the family to come along immediately. If elderly or sick people were in bed sleeping, they emptied a bucket of cold water over them and dragged them into the street in their pajamas. Neighbors had their curtains closed and didn't see anything. The terror intensified.

The Dutch police assisted the German police with arresting the Jews at their homes. Some Dutch officers though, let their "targets" get away by warning them in advance.

***

The trains ran mostly on schedule. If there was a shortage of trains, they were made to wait in a theater guarded by German and Dutch SS soldiers. The Germans paid for the "rental" of the theater with monies stolen from Jewish bank accounts.

The auditorium and orchestra chairs had been ripped out and placed alongside the walls. It was packed with crying and screaming kids, whining children wanting to go home, and frustrated parents waiting for their names to be called so they could start on their journey to an unknown destination in Poland.

Some families were there for hours, others days. There were no shower and the toilets were filthy. There was no toilet paper, and food and water were in short supply. Everyone was tense, anxious facing the unknown.

JC staff wore armbands. Herman didn't always. He knew the theater guards and he came and went greeting them without his armband. They thought he was one of them. A few times, he walked someone past the guard, right out of the building.

Inside the theater, he helped where he could. He took last-minute scribbles and promised to deliver them.

On a Sunday in June in 1942, the Council mailed out the first batch of envelopes containing orders to report. Last names A through D under the age of forty were first.

Two days later, at around 10:30 am, Sonja was at work when the phone rang.

Her mother cried, "Your notice to report arrived in the mail today, one for you and one for our Judie. Uncle Philip came by to tell us that Sara and Beppie are also leaving."

Sonja reacted immediately. "Let me get a hold of Herman."

"Herman? Are you still seeing him after we..."

"Mother I love him. Let's not waste time."

"Can he stop this?"

"Perhaps he can. I'll pick them up from you."

"Your father is already on his way to you."

The moment Sonja hung up, the phone rang again. Herman sounded agitated.

"We can't meet for lunch today. There's a big roundup going on. Even people with exemption stamps are being arrested. I've got to stay and help them."

She told him about the notices for her and her sister.

"Tell you mom not to worry. Bring them to me as soon as you can, but stay away from downtown. Tell your dad too."

"I love you."

"See you later."

She hung up, and the door opened. Her dad entered. He quickly closed the door behind him and handed her the two envelopes. She noticed he looked pale. She told him that Herman he might be able to help.

Jacob hesitated. "Can we accept that after everything that's happened?"

"Of course dad, doesn't everything happen for a reason, remember?"

He faintly smiled, and told her to be safe.

"Stay away from downtown today."

He kissed her gently on her forehead and left. She put on her coat.

A surge of adrenaline rushed through her as she used her purse to cover the yellow star. Herman worked across town. She saw a horse pulling a cart that belonged to the company her father had used for shipping his fabrics. She asked the driver if she could hitch a ride under the canvas.

Anxiously, she sat amongst the parcels. It seemed to take forever. She peeked out and recognized the Beethovenstraat. When the cart stopped, she jumped and kept running until she reached Herman's office.

It was hectic inside. The hallways were crowded and noisy. Nobody knew where Herman was. She decided to wait. By four o'clock, when she was about to leave the envelopes with a young man who promised to pass them on to Herman, she saw him through the crowded hallway, making his way toward her.

She gave him the envelopes.

"Everything's fine, Son. Tell your mom not to worry. I'm sorry, but I couldn't help your cousins. They have to go. Tell your uncle not see them off to the station."

Someone called his name.

"I've got to go. I'll call you later."

He kissed her quickly and disappeared into the crowd.

That evening, she told her parents not to worry. Her mom cried. Her own daughters didn't have to leave, but her nieces did. And so did everyone else between the ages of five and twenty-five. Long after bedtime, they arrived at Camp Westerbork, unaware of how much worse things were going to get.

Over a cup of tea, the Rabbi suggested letting Sonja and Herman marry.

"Lots of couples are getting married. At least with the same last name, they will stay together. Also, if Herman is your son-in-law, you'll be fine to accept his help."

Sonja, not usually at a loss for words, was speechless when she heard the good news. How could she ever thank her parents and the Rabbi?

They were married during a civil ceremony with some forty other couples, in August of 1942. It was a frugal event and they were not the happiest of times but she was thrilled to be Herman's wife. They wanted to honeymoon a few days at her uncle's in the South, but leaving Amsterdam was against the law and not even Herman's papers could safeguard them. She didn't mind. He promised her a honeymoon after the war. He was taking her to America. They had the rest of their lives to celebrate. After cake and coffee, they went back to work.

Sonja and Herman moved in with Mr. and Mrs. Gans, friends of her parents. They had plenty of room because both their sons had moved out. Mrs. Gans refused their rent check and insisted they share their meals together, like a family.

Herman's work gave Mrs. Gans a sense of security. A copy of their wedding photo was strategically placed in the living room. Sonja often looked at it, remembering the downstairs neighbor of her parents.

There were rumors that Herman was the man for an exemption stamp. He worked the lists, removed names. Sonja's parents never received their notices. Herman had signed Sluzker's name on their exemption letter.

Liliane Pelzman

Order to report

*Order to report included exactly what to bring on your
trip: 1 suitcase or backpack, 1 pair of rubber boots, 2 pair of
socks, 2 pieces of underwear, 2 shirts, 1 pair of work pants, 2
woolen blankets, 2 sets of sheets, 1 bowl, 1 mug, 1 spoon and
1 sweater, towel and toiletries.*
  NO LIVE ANIMALS

7. Hiding

The police had received an anonymous complaint. They had dragged a woman out of bed, and out of the house in her pajamas. She didn't want to go and kept screaming. She woke up the whole neighborhood, the letter writer complained.
"Look, if you have to pick'm up, can't you at least control them so they don't wake up the entire neighborhood."

Jews on their way to the station

***

Cousin Judy was going to hide. She visited Jacob and Jet, and wanted to take Sonja's little sister with her.

"No way. That's far too dangerous," her mom had said.

"You're jeopardizing all of us. Perhaps it's better if you don't come back here. This is way too dangerous."

For the first time in her life, she heard her dad oppose her mom.

"You will always be welcome in our home."

Even though Herman came home late every night, these were relatively happy months. Without realizing it, by marrying Herman Rosenstein, Sonja had moved from the C to the R on the list of deportations because the names were alphabetized, thereby delaying her fate.

She often dropped in on her parents, even though walking was dangerous. She had asked Herman for an exemption stamp but he'd told her not to worry. Especially now that they were married, she was safe, he had told her.

Mrs. Gans knew of a hiding place for Sonja's sister. After thinking it over, her parents agreed. But Judie was having a hard time. She was forced to eat pork, and she cried a lot. Jet missed her youngest daughter too much, and decided to bring her back home.

Sonja's mom collected their most valuable belongings and gave them for safe keeping to Mrs. Roderigues, their housekeeper. With the neighbors watching her coming and going, it had become too dangerous for this brave woman to keep working for Jet. They cried when they hugged good-bye.

On Sonja's birthday, Mrs. Gans and Sonja were in the living room when the bell rang. It was her dad. He was alone.

"It's too far for your mother to walk. Happy birthday from both of us."

Her dad told them that a police officer had come by to take them away, but he saw their wedding photo and asked, "Who is that? I know that guy."

"That's my son-in-law and my daughter," her mother had answered.

"Is that right? Well, good day, then. Come on," he had said to his partner. "We're at the wrong address."

"They left, but your mother is terribly worried."

He looked worried too.

Jet decided to have her polio foot operated on, for their upcoming trip. Fourteen days later, she was released from the hospital. She walked a little better, which made her feel more confident and optimistic about the future.

Sonja, little Judie, and their parents, 1933

Sonja's parents, 1939

1940

Gerdi & Emile en Sonja & Herman
Gerdi & Emile and Sonja & Herman

For more images please visit the website
www.neversurrender.me

Judie and Sonja (R), 1941

Amsterdam - Jews only Quarter, 1941

Sonja's father Jacob was murdered in
concentration camp Sobibor in 1943

8. Problem solved

Wives and mothers discussed ways of getting their husbands and sons back. One son overheard the conversation and suddenly grasped the truth behind the men disappearing.

"I'll be back," he told his mother and his sister.

He disappeared and went into hiding. The son survived and never forgave himself for not saving his mother and his sister.

For the Nazis, the Jewish problem in the Netherlands was solved. One hundred and five thousand Jewish men, women, and children were deported. At the end of the war in 1945, five had thousand survived.

Jews on their way to the train station

***

Herman still did not realize what was happening to the families that were being deported to "the East." He was told that they were going to work. But what about the babies, the grandparents? Sick people couldn't work?

Walking to work had become too dangerous, so when Sonja surrendered her bike, she had to give up her job. She asked Herman if he knew of any jobs in the neighborhood. He arranged for her a typing job at the Jewish Council, right around the corner.

9. Herman arrested

The major told his captain to accelerate the deportations. He recruited volunteers, and paid them to find Jews. A group of volunteers traveled throughout Holland and caught some 8500 men, women, children, and babies.

Jews were imprisoned in camp Westerbork, a transit camp near the German border, before they were sent on to their final destination.

Between 1942 and 1944, almost every Tuesday a train left for the concentration camps Auschwitz, Sobibór, Bergen-Belsen, and Theresienstadt. The Nazis used monies from Jewish bank accounts to pay the Dutch Railway System. For the Jews they bought one-way tickets; for the guards they bought return tickets. Trains ran on a tight schedule. Dutch Railway System shares skyrocketed.

In 2005, the Dutch Railway System apologized for its role in the deportation of Jews. Modern historians have suggested that without the mass collaboration of the railway companies in Europe, the Final Solution would not have been possible.

Train station Westerbork, 1943

***

April 1943. On a hot summer evening, when they were having dinner, a car came to a screeching halt. They held their breath. They heard approaching footsteps, then banging on the front door.

"Open up!"

Should they or not without Herman there? Worried, Mr. Gans opened the door. Two Dutch police officers pushed him aside and entered.

"Check the cellar," said the one giving orders. His partner disappeared. The man entered the living room, looked around, and noticed silverware on the table. He grabbed the forks and knives, wiped them clean on the white tablecloth, and slid them into his coat pocket. He moved to the cupboard, grabbed a handful of silverware from a drawer, and slid that into his other pocket. His partner returned from the cellar with a canning jar. His boss nodded that it was ok for him to take it.

"Come on. Come along."

"There must be a mix-up. I work at the JC. This is my husband." Sonja motioned to her wedding photo.

"None of my business. They'll figure it out over there at the theater."

While their papers were checked at the entrance, Sonja asked a JC staff member if Herman was in the building. A few minutes later, Herman came rushing toward them.

"Wait here! Don't enter the auditorium. Once you're inside, they won't let you leave."

Before she could tell him that Mr. and Mrs. Gans were with her, he disappeared into the busy hallway. Moments later, he returned with a young man in a German SS uniform.

"This is Günter. He is taking you home. Hurry. I'll see you tonight." Günter escorted them out of the building and drove them home. In the car on the way home, Mr. and Mrs. Gans decided to go into hiding.

At home, Mrs. Gans grabbed their backpacks. She told Sonja to come with them.

"I can't leave without Herman." They hugged.

"Take good care of yourself."

Moments later, Mr. and Mrs. Gans pulled the front door shut and disappeared. She was alone. Jumpy at the slightest sound, she waited for Herman.

When Herman came home late that night, she told him that Mr. and Mrs. Gans had gone into hiding.

"What's going to happen to us?"

"We'll be fine. They need us."

He believed that they should move in case the police came back for Mr. and Mrs. Gans. He had friends who had a room for rent and he suggested moving there.

Sonja packed a tube of toothpaste, a bottle of shampoo, her beloved photo album, a few summer dresses made from her father's fabrics, and the postcards her father had sent from his many trips. With only two backpacks, the move was easy. Herman told her to take her backpack to work just in case. At the same time, he put her at ease, insisting again that everything was going to be fine.

"Don't worry." Those were his exact words.

In May, the captain left town for a business trip to Berlin. The major initiated a huge roundup, and decided to see for himself. The phone rang at the new address in the Rijnstraat. Herman sounded anxious.

"There's a round up near the Meijer Square. I'm going there to see if I can help. I'll be home late."

"Please be careful," she said nervously.

The square was crowded with uniforms: regular police, Dutch SS, German SS, Gestapo, Green Police, so called because of their green uniforms and the Order Police.

As soon as the victims saw Herman, they rushed over to him. He did not want to attract attention and tried to calm them down. He got his lists out, checked their names, and assured them, "I'll see what I can do."

The major was watching from a distance. He saw the commotion and walked over, followed by several SS men. "What's going on here? What are you doing? Who are you?"

Herman told him he worked for Aus der Fünten and there'd been a mistake.

"These people have been wrongly detained. They all have exemption stamps." He held up the list. Lages grabbed the list from his hand, tore it up, and accused Herman of sabotage.

She waited up all night. The following morning, earlier than usual, she went to the office.

"Herman is in jail. Lages himself arrested him yesterday," her boss told her.

Sonja was frantic and wanted to go and visit him, but her boss warned her that she might be arrested if she tried.

A couple of weeks later, Herman was deported to Camp Westerbork, a concentration camp in Holland, not far from the German border, where most Jews were sent before leaving for Poland.

He was held in the punishment barracks for criminals who had committed a crime, which was distinct from simply being Jewish. His aunt Betty and her daughter Jenny were already at there, as were Feli and Jack, two uncles. They had been there since 1938.

June 20th, some four weeks later. It was a warm Sunday morning. Holland had been occupied by Nazi Germany for three years now. At around ten-thirty, Sonja walked to work. Her mind was with her beloved brand new husband Herman. When was she going to see him again? It had been four longs weeks since his arrest.

All of a sudden, a car and a truck screamed into the street from opposite ends and came to a screeching halt. The sound of shrill whistles suddenly filled the peaceful street. About ten police officers with angry barking dogs jumped from the back of the truck and ran up to anybody wearing a yellow star. SS men motioned spectators to move on.

The driver of the truck saw Sonja's star on her coat. "Papers," he barked at her.

She handed him her ID.

"Come on, get in."

Terrified she climbed into the back of the truck. Men, women, and a few children sat packed side-by-side on facing benches. They made room. The driver dropped the canvas cover and climbed behind the wheel. She heard him say, "We've got enough of them for now." He was referring to the Jews quota for the day.

He drove them to the soccer field on the Olympia Square, a block from her office. At the entrance, behind a row of tables, Jewish prisoners from Camp Westerbork were registering the new "load."

"ID! Address? Front door keys!"

She saw a guy she knew from the Jewish Committee, helping an elderly couple with their suitcases. When he was done, she called him.

She asked him if he could pick up her backpack from the office.

Half an hour later, he returned.

"Your parents and your sister came through here earlier today. They left a couple of hours ago. You'll see them there."

She thanked him, but he barely heard her. He was already busy with the next person. She was ordered to wait and sat down on the grass, calmed somewhat by the news. She thought, "So I'll travel a bit. It is different from Zandvoort, and at least I am able to work."

She searched through her backpack and was pleased with her dresses and so very happy she had stuck her photo album in. She looked at a photo of Herman. Yes, she almost felt relieved now. Herman was in Westerbork. A few more hours and they would be together again. To avoid creasing her dresses, she rolled them up tightly.

After a couple of hours, they were ordered into the back of a truck and were driven to the strain station. No one said a word. At the station, the group of fifty or sixty people walked towards the train. Some carrying only a backpack, others dragging suitcases.

A policeman walking next to her, whispered, "Girl, take off your yellow star. Rip it off. Let me take you home. Don't be afraid. I will take care of you."

He kept insisting.

"Don't get into that train. Tear off that star."

"I want to go to my husband."

She whispered, looking at the ground ahead of her.

"Take it off while you still can and come with me."

She thought, if she went with him, he'd report her to the police.

"I am married; I am going to my husband in Westerbork."

"Don't get onto that train. Listen to me!"

She hesitated.

"But what if the police...?"

"I am the police."

She could hardly move. Children and babies were yelling and crying. More and more people were pushed into her car—suitcases, backpacks, and blankets. The cattle car was packed. She sweated abundantly. The sliding door was shut. She heard the clank of the bolt being secured. The locomotive with its fifteen or so cattle cars jolted and started moving slowly. How did she get here? How did she end up in a cattle car on her way to Westerbork?

It was dark and dirty. Do not drop your purse, she told herself, or you'll be trampled.

Her eyes adjusted to the darkness. A woman next to her said, "At least the fear of being caught is gone. Tonight I can finally sleep."

She agreed, "There's something to that."

The sound of every click-clack, click-clack brought her closer to Herman.

When they arrived at the camp, they were handed over to camp personnel, Jewish prisoners themselves.

10. Westerbork

Concentration Camp Westerbork came about on an isolated plain in the northeast of the country, when 3000 German Jews applied for refugee status in Holland before the Nazis invaded.

The people that lived there were refugees and they were in charge of the day-to-day operations of the camp. Personnel, barracks leaders, kitchen personnel, mail carriers, cleaners, and camp police all had to be managed, scheduled, and supervised.

They spoke German, which obviously was an advantage. They lived in small, one- and two-bedroom cabins and were allowed to leave the camp on travel passes only if they had relatives or friends that they wanted to visit. They had to report back before sundown. They had no working permits.

When the Nazis took over, the refugee camp became a transit camp.

Fast forward to 1942. Dutch Jews started to arrive. They all wanted to work because they knew that working stalled being deported. Jobs in the administration office, hospital, or outside the camp, working the fields growing potatoes, rye, oats, wheat, and beets, were most popular. Herman's uncles Feli and Jack were early residents. They had been there since 1938.

You could take classes or play sports. Even shopping was somewhat possible. The camp used camp money in its "store" or "canteen."

There was a kindergarten, and the older kids were required to take classes until the age of fifteen. Sometimes the Tuesday train deported too many teachers and lessons were canceled. It took a while before new teachers arrived and classes started again. While the food was not any good and camp hygiene was terrible, the number of deaths compared to other camps, was relatively low.

Even though breaking the rules was punished, Westerbork was bearable, especially if you were a patient in the hospital. The hospital beds were more comfortable than the bunk beds in the barracks.

Westerbork was proud of its hospital that counted over 1725 beds, and 120 doctors, 1000 men and women personnel, all Jewish prisoners. Those who were too ill to make the long journey were admitted to the hospital. Once declared fit, they were placed on the next deportation.

The last train left Amsterdam at the end of September 1943. On board were the members of the Jewish Council. They had been unable to save themselves.

Camp Westerbork 1943

***

It was dark out when the locomotive came to a juddering stop. Sonja felt tired and dirty, but it had been worth it. She's going to be with Herman.

The door slid open.

"Get out. Get out," instructions echoed along the train.

With slightly more than a thousand people, they were herded to the registration barracks and ordered to wait. Soon the hall was packed and lines were forming outside.

Grandmothers, grandfathers, aunts and uncles, parents, children, crying babies, brothers, sisters, sick and disabled people, everybody rested on the floor amidst their luggage, waiting to be registered. Doctors were making sure people were all right.

Behind a long row of tables, prisoners typed information cards.

It took hours before it was Sonja's turn. While waiting, she saw her uncle Anton in the crowd rushing toward her. He kissed her. She was surprised to see him. He had gone into hiding with his wife. He had no time to explain and quickly told her that he worked in the hospital and that her parents and sister arrived a few trains earlier.

"I admitted your mother and Mientje (his other sister) to the hospital."

"What about Herman?"

He knew nothing about Herman and disappeared into the chaos.

Sonja saw Sol, one of her cousins and pushed her way towards him. He was busy but kissed her and told her that her parents and sister arrived a little while ago.

"What about Herman? What do you know about Herman?"

He shook his head apologetically and hurried to a typist who was calling him.

Finally, it was her turn.

"Name. Place of birth? Last address? Keys? Profession? Family?" the typist asked. She was told not to hide any money, so she handed over the little bit of cash she carried on her.

Moments later, someone called out, "Sonja Rosenstein, Barracks 65!"

Barracks 65 was packed with triple bunk beds facing each other across a narrow aisle. The beds were so closely stacked that they were accessible from the aisle only. Sonja got a top bunk near the door. That night she found out that the light in the corridor would stay on all night and shine right on her face.

For a moment, she sat still, taking it all in—the noise, the open suitcases, the clothes everywhere. A young mother and her two children were dressed as if they were going on vacation. She started to itch. There were fleas everywhere.

Her neighbor in the next bed filled her in on the rules and regulations of the camp. Be inside your barracks by eight o'clock, in bed by ten o'clock. Breakfast was a piece of bread and was at eight o'clock.

She left her backpack on the bed and went to the hospital in search of her mother and aunts.

On her way, she ran into her father pushing a wheelbarrow. He had lost weight. She cried as she ran up to him.

"No need to cry," he said, and repeated as he had many times before, "everything happens for a reason. We must have faith, now more than ever. It's going to be fine. Go visit your mom."

The hospital seemed chaotic. She first found Anton's wife aunt Jet.

"We were hiding but someone turned us in for a reward."

Sonja hugged her and asked if she knew where her mother was. When she found her mother, they hugged.

"I just saw dad and aunt Jet. How are you? Where's Judie?"

Sonja found her little sister on the floor in a dirty barracks, fighting an asthma attack. A few days later, Anton admitted her sister to the hospital.

Uncle Feli and Jack had arranged a job for Jenny, Herman's cousin, in the admin office. Jenny told Sonja that Herman was in solitary, and that she was trying to get him transferred to the hospital. It took her three weeks to get him finally admitted into the hospital. A few days later, according to plan, Anton diagnosed Herman healthy and he was allowed to stay at the cabin with his uncles. Sonja visited a lot.

Herman's uncle Feli got Sonja a bread-buttering job in the kitchen for a while. After that, she joined a cleaning crew.

She mopped and cleaned every morning from seven to ten. She spent a few hours in the hospital visiting with her mom, her aunts, and her sister. She kept Herman for the afternoon, evening and night. Quiet moments before the storm; they were oblivious to how the next chapter of their lives was going to play out.

The camp commander received instructions on how many Jews he needed to deport that week. He left the details up to the committee of early residents. They decided who was leaving. The committee met every Monday and discussed logistics like how many people went into a cattle car, car representatives, and which doctors were to accompany the transport.

Tuesday morning, between two and three am, the barracks leaders announced the names of those leaving. People packed and said their good-byes.

Early morning, all those leaving were required to line up inside their barracks with their belongings, ready to go. CaPo's (Camp Police) fetched them and corralled them to the platform. Some families left together, others were separated. Imagine the drama with the kids.

Sonja saw her cousin Sara looking for an empty bunk, there were none. She called Sara's name. Sara's face lit up and made her way through the commotion towards Sonja. They hugged and Sonja insisted that Sara share her bunk. Fourteen days they spent together before Sara's name was read from the list.

That Tuesday morning, with her backpack ready to go, Sara said, "We won't ever forget these last days, eh, Sonja? When this is all over, we will catch up."

They kissed and Sara was gone. Three days later, Sara was dead.

Sonja's all-time favorite book since elementary school was *The Clog Maker and the Princess*. Obsessed with the story, she got the book on her tenth birthday. How happy she'd been when she opened her present.

The story went like this: The princess could not find a pair of shoes that fitted her, so her dad, the king, held a competition. Whoever made shoes that fit his daughter would be well rewarded. A poor forester made a pair of wooden clogs. The fronts of the clogs were painted to look like a dwarf's beard. The dwarf was painted wearing a red cap. The forester went to the palace. The clogs fit, and the forester ended up a wealthy man. She must have read the book a thousand times.

Sonja had brought a pair of pretty pumps from Amsterdam, but winters in Westerbork were muddy affairs. She told a carpenter about *The Clog Maker and the Princess*, describing the clogs in detail and asked him to make her a pair of wooden shoes. A few days later, she picked up a pair of lemon-yellow clogs with a dwarf and a beard painted on them. She cried. She was homesick, missing her parents, her sister, missing her life as she remembered it.

June 28, 1943. Sonja and Herman visited her mom and the other family members in the hospital every day, but they weren't sick and Anton couldn't keep them in the hospital any longer.

"Father and I are leaving tomorrow. Judie is coming with us," her mom told Sonja on Monday,

Sonja kissed her mom good-bye.

"I love you mom. We're going to be fine, right?"

She kissed here again. And again.

"Silly girl, we'll be seeing each other soon."

"Herman thinks so too."

"We've grown very fond of him. Your dad and I..."

"I hope they're ok," she said to Herman in the cabin the following morning, as they heard the train rolling out of the station.

"Don't cry. Trust me, this war won't go on for much longer."

That day, her mom and dad, her sister and her aunt were deported like cattle to their slaughter with nearly 2400 people other people.

There were rumors that deported Jews were murdered. She asked uncle Jack if all those people on the train were going to be killed.

"My dear, please? Do not believe everything you hear."

Rumor had it that Theresienstadt was not so bad. But Sobibor? Her stomach heaved.

Somebody had escaped from jail. The major traveled to Westerbork to investigate.

He discovered that Herman Rosenstein, the young man who he had personally arrested some months earlier was still in Westerbork. He was furious. What was Aus der Funten's protégé still doing in Holland?

He wanted him sent on the next train to Auschwitz immediately. The following morning, the major returned to Amsterdam, thinking Herman was on his way to Auschwitz.

11. The End of the Beginning

Thanks to the excellent record keeping by the Nazis, we know many years later that on that particular Tuesday morning in June of 1943, exactly 2,397 mothers, fathers, uncles, aunts, sons, daughters, nieces, nephews, cousins and grandkids were deported to a concentration camp called Sobibor. They were gassed immediately upon arrival. Sonja's parents, her sister and her aunt were amongst them. They didn't stand a chance.

Deportation 1943, Camp Westerbork

***

One morning in August, the CaPo's (camp police) were working up a sweat loading backpacks, suitcases, and other personal possessions into eighty packed cattle cars. Sonja and Herman were the last to climb aboard. They had been married exactly one year.

Six years earlier, a court in Amsterdam had convicted a farmer for transporting fifteen cows instead of fourteen in one car. Was that door even going to close? CaPo's were rushing alongside the train, using chalk to write the number of persons on the doors of each car.

Sitting on bare floorboards, cramped, with a bucket of water in the corner and an empty bucket next to it, they were on their way to Auschwitz. The ramp, an hour earlier a madhouse, was calm now. On the platform, lists were checked and double-checked in typical orderly German fashion. The doors of the cattle cars were bolted shut.

Herman's uncles cried in the distance as they watch them disappear behind the sliding door. Suddenly, approaching from the far end of the platform, voices were heard yelling, "Herman and Sonja Rosenstein! Herman and Sonja Rosenstein."

Staff members were running past the cars, trying to locate them.

"Herman and Sonja Rosenstein! Herman and Sonja Rosenstein! In which car are you?"

"Over here!"

"Oh, God." Someone behind them moaned.

"They are getting out."

"Herman and Sonja Rosenstein!"

"We're over here!"

They heard the door unbolt. It slid open a tiny bit. A young CaPo stood on the platform, holding a list.

"Herman Rosenstein?"

"Yes."

"You and your wife follow me. Quickly!"

They could barely make it out sideways. As Sonja jumped out, she remembered her backpack.

She turned around, but the door was already closed.

"My clothes! My photo album! Our wedding photos!"

Herman squeezed her hand and guided her away from the train. Jenny waited for them inside the administration barracks. She cried as she hugged them. She explained the major and the commandant of the camp had an argument and Herman's fate had inadvertently become a matter of prestige. Wanting to show who was in charge, the commandant ordered them off the train and approved Jenny's request to send her cousin and his wife to Theresienstadt.

From the cabin, they heard "their" train leave the station.

"What's going to happen to us?"

"The Americans are not going to let this maniac go on for much longer. Trust me."

The following Tuesday Rabbi de Hond and his family were leaving. She had known the Rabbi her whole life. He had always been there for her. Have I thanked him enough? Thanks to him, they'd been allowed to marry. His wife and his children were all being sent on. She made sure to say good-bye. He smiled when he saw her approach through the commotion. He placed his hands on her head and blessed her one last time. Dear Rabbi de Hond. Three days later, he, his wife, and his kids were dead.

February 25, 1944. Six o'clock in the morning. The weather was icy cold. Against the rules, they woke up together in the cabin. An old, run-down passenger train to Theresienstadt was scheduled to leave at eleven o'clock. Sonja was nervous. Herman tried to set her at ease.

"It's going to be fine." He told her there are rumors that the Americans are planning something. You'll see. It's almost over."

She had a hard time believing him.

"As long as we can stay together."

They kissed and she left to fetch her belongings. She did not own much after she left her backpack on the train. One friend had given her a dress, another a sweater.

She said goodbye to Jenny. Jenny's mother, her brother, and his wife had already left. Now that Herman and Sonja were leaving, Jenny only had her two uncles left. In September, the three of them would be deported to Auschwitz.

The passenger train was packed with exactly 911 persons aboard. There were forty people in a car with seating for twenty-four. Before the train started moving, the toilets were already filthy.

Sonja sat on Herman's lap. The commandant rode his bike along the length of the train. When he made an abrupt motion with his hand, the train groaned into motion. Suddenly, there were voices calling from the platform.

"Are they calling us? No, that can't be true."

The ominous whistle blew. The train rolled slowly out of Camp Westerbork. At least she was with Herman. She leaned her head on his shoulder.

"I'll love you as long as I live," she heard him whisper in her ear before she dosed off.

Reports were sent to the Allied governments in London and Washington. They included detailed accounts of Auschwitz-Birkenau: the number of transports per day, the layout of the camps, sketches of the gas chambers, and so forth. These reports lead to some politicians wanting to bomb the camps and the railways. But the British and the United States rejected the idea. The official explanation given by Congress was that a diversion of substantial resources to win the Jewish battle was unacceptable. Those resources were needed to win the war.

After three days, the train arrived in Theresienstadt. Sonja and Herman belonged to the 4,597 privileged Jews for whom the East meant Theresienstadt, for now.

12. Theresienstadt

In what used to be Czechoslovakia, about forty miles northwest of the capital of Prague, the Austrian emperor Jozef II built an army fortification and named it Terezin, after his mother Maria Theresa. The fortification was comprised of a small and a bigger fortress. The bigger fortress included ten garrisons. Each garrison was three stories high and contained an inner courtyard. They turned the big fortress into a concentration camp and kept the small fortress as a prison.

The Nazis changed the Czech name to the German name of Theresienstadt. Originally, Terezin could house six thousand people. By the end of 1943, it housed fifty-eight thousand.

Overpopulation had its consequences. Lice and typhoid were serious problems. There was no water or toilet paper. Toilets were filthy. Taking a shower was expensive. Washing just about belonged to the past. Delousing crews sprayed regularly, but that didn't help.

There was a strict camp hierarchy. Here, too, Jews were in charge of Jews. In Theresienstadt, the Czech Jews were in charge.

From the unventilated attics with spiders and rats, to the unpaved floors in the cellars, newly arrived prisoners tried to find a space to lie down and call their own. Thousands of lives connected during moments of chaos.

Flanked by Czech guards, new arrivals were taken to the registration center and ordered to fill out forms asking about their education and work experience. All remaining valuables were seized and sold in 'shops'.

Concentration camp Theresienstadt

***

Sonja and Herman were assigned to the Hamburger barracks.

She landed in Room 112. Herman's room was one floor up. Sonja's room housed twelve double bunk beds for twenty-four Czech women. One of her roommates explained the camp's hierarchy in German; whom to trust, whom to stay away from, what was allowed, and what wasn't. She was told where to report for work the next day.

They gave her a blouse and a pair of dark brown overalls, and she was put her to work in a ten men and women cleaning crew. Every ten days, they were assigned to clean a different location; the hospital, the admin offices, etc. Everyone wanted to work in the bakery because Theresienstadt meant going hungry. Herman talked to the baker and got her a job. Her day started at six a.m. First, she went to a large washroom that had a long sink with a row of faucets above it. She made do with a couple drops of cold water. Then she hurried to the bakery.

The bakery detail started at seven o'clock. They taught her how to knead bread, how to place the loaves in the oven, when to take them out, and how to make them look shiny. When the loaves were ready, she dropped them off at the distribution windows throughout the camp. At the end of the day, the baker nodded at her, giving her permission to take the leftover bread. She couldn't let anybody see her. Being caught meant deportation to Auschwitz.

During one of her shifts, she got her hands on a small bag of flour. She wanted to make tiny pancakes on the stove in her room. When her shift was over, she hid the bag in her underpants. On the way to her building, the bag started to leak, leaving a Hansel and Gretchen like trail. The girls behind her warned her. She pretended to have sudden stinging pains in her side. They laced their fingers together and carried her. The tiny pancakes were delicious.

Like the other married women, Sonja sneaked off to visit Herman whenever she had a chance. Often she brought him bread.

Herman worked in the agriculture detail. He worked long hours. From seven in the morning to six in the evening, his agri-detail worked on a piece of land outside the camp, growing all sorts of vegetables for German consumption only.

He was in good condition. He worked hard and looked healthy, even though he started feeling pangs of hunger. The men in his work detail liked him. So did the guards.

Every day, after her shift, she'd go to the top of a hill and waited for Herman's detail to return to camp. She touched a piece of bread in her pocket she'd saved for him.

Feeling tired, she dozed off. She saw her dad having breakfast, her mother cutting him a piece of gingerbread.

Her sister was telling them a funny story about something that happened at school. They all laughed, but she was dying to leave to meet Herman. Boy, that breakfast on the table sure looked good!

The sound of footsteps woke her. Herman's detail was marching by, without Herman.

"He's in jail," a friend in his detail told her later.

"One of the guards noticed his sleeves dangling. He'd sewed them shut and filled them with vegetables for you."

She was terrified. She had never felt as alone as at that moment.

While Herman was in jail, she tried to stay busy by welcoming trains arriving from Holland. Recognizing a familiar face in the crowd gave her a momentary sense of relief, and vice versa.

A cousin of her mom's stepped off the train.

"Uncle Ben, it's so good to see you."

They hugged.

"How are things here?" He noticed she had lost weight.

"It's horrible. Herman's in jail and there's little to eat."

"Are you hungry? Do you want a sandwich? I've saved it from Westerbork. It's yours if you want it."

He handed her the sandwich.

She wolfed it down.

"The cheese is delicious."

"That's not cheese," he said, "the butter must have spoiled."

He went through the registration routine and when he was done, she was waiting for him. As she walked him to his assigned building, they filled each other in.

"I am on my way to Switzerland."

Ben was a violinist and had gotten a pass, thanks to the conductor of the Amsterdam Philharmonic who had used his German connections.

She knew a person who knew a person who knew a German in charge, and a few days later Herman was out of jail.

"When we're back in Amsterdam, I have to tell you something important," Herman told her that evening.

"Why not tell me now?"

"I want to wait until this is all behind us and we are back in Amsterdam."

She did not insist.

June 6 1944 was Decision Day or D-day, as we know it. American and British troops landed on the west coast of France. For a while, there were no deportations. The prisoners breathed slightly easier. The following month Claus von Stauffenberg tried to kill Hitler, but failed. The rumors of the attempt and the landing in France filled the prisoners with hope.

The Nazis coordinated a propaganda campaign to show the world that the prisoners in Theresienstadt had nothing to complain about. The Red Cross was coming to inspect the camp. The center underwent a metamorphosis. Buildings were painted. Parks, playgrounds, and cafés were constructed. Tablecloths and flowers in little vases decorated the café tables. Windows on the downstairs floor were beautified with flowerpots and curtains. Rumors spread like wildfire that on behalf of the international community, committee delegates of the International Red Cross were coming to visit. The Jewish Orchestra conducted by Rafael Schächter started practicing Verdi's Requiem. Prisoners received bigger food rations. Children received special attention; a playground was built, complete with sand boxes, kiddy baths, swings, and rocking horses. When the day approached of the delegation's visit, the streets were cleaned and the sidewalk scrubbed with water and soap.

Answers were rehearsed. Prisoners who refused to cooperate were locked up. Kurt Gerron, a famous producer, director, actor who fled from Germany to Holland where the Nazis caught up with him all the same, was responsible for entertainment. Gerron assembled a choir and started rehearsing the choir in the Maagdenburger barracks.

Herman told Kurt Gerron about Sonja's beautiful coloratura soprano voice and arranged an audition during a rehearsal break. So much had happened, her nerves were frazzled and her voice failed her. She cleared her throat and tried again, but it was no good. She apologized and Herman thanked Gerron for his time. He could tell she started to unravel emotionally.

Walking back through the playground, she cried as he tried to cheer her up. His voice was warm and his firm arm around her shoulder made her feel an intense love for him.

"I'd go crazy without you here."

He kissed her tears. He stopped walking and looked into her eyes. He told her not to worry and that everything was going to work out. He was convinced that the Americans were going to show up eventually.

"One day, we'll live in America, our kids will be all grown up, and we'll look back and remember how we got through this together. Remember what you dad used to say. Everything happens for a reason."

They walked back to their barracks holding hands. In the playground, amidst kids playing as if life couldn't get any better than this, he stopped and looked into her eyes.

"Come and watch me play soccer this afternoon. My first goal will be for you."

Maurice Rossel was a twenty-six-year-old Swiss national, who represented the Red Cross. He and two Danish government officials came to see the situation in the camp. They came upon a scene comparable to a movie set. The smallest details had been taken care of. The prisoners were warned not to come too close to the visitors or they would face deportation. They still did not know what that meant exactly, but it sounded dreadful enough.

That Friday they felt like normal people. Over the last couple of days, they'd been given a little more food than usual and that Friday they were allowed to stroll outside. Maurice Rossel took pictures and in his report, he noted that the conditions in Theresienstadt were reasonable and that nobody lacked for anything.

The day after Rossel's visit, Kurt Gerron, the orchestra, and the choir for which Sonja had tried out were deported to Auschwitz. Three days later, they were all dead, killed in gas chambers. Sonja and Herman didn't know that at the time.

Two weeks later, another 11,000 prisoners left for the gas chambers on their last train ride.

Only after the war facts revealed that thousands of prisoners had died of starvation and disease in concentration camp Theresienstadt.

13. From Bad to Worse

August 25, 1944. The Americans liberated Paris. When word reached the camp, the prisoners thought the war would be over soon. But it would take another nine months for the war in Europe to be over.

Theresienstadt remained a transit camp to the ovens of Auschwitz. Tens of thousands of prisoners were dying from starvation and dehydration. The lack of food and water and the squalid living situation took its toll.

Americans liberate Paris

***

They needed a thousand men to help build a new camp somewhere. They were told that it was only temporary. They'd be reunited with their wives soon again. Herman was called up to leave. They stayed awake all night and talked.

"When am I going to get to see you again?"

"I wish I knew. As soon as the war is over, go back to Amsterdam. I'll find you there. I promise."

Soldiers ordered him to keep walking.

"I'll wait for you."

"Remember the good times. Always remember the good times."

He blew her one last kiss before he and Jimmy, a friend from Holland, boarded the train together with some thousand men. She felt scared. Uncle Ben had left for Switzerland, and now Herman was gone.

Again, she went to the platform and waited for arriving trains hoping to see someone she knew. Again, she was lucky.

Gerdi, Emile, and his mother were passing through and were on their way to Switzerland. Emile asked about Herman. She told them what happened. While they were waiting to register, Emile was eying the ground.

"Are we coming back here?"

Sonja shook her head.

"Why?"

Gerdi and Emile nodded at each other, quickly squatted down, and dug a hole in the ground. In the blink of an eye, Emile stuck a pouch with cash into the hole. They stamped the sand and carefully studied the location.

"It's all we have left for when we get to Switzerland," Emile explained.

Before long, guards herded them into the registration building. A few days later, Emile returned, found the spot, and dug up the pouch.

"You are going to your husbands," an SS captain announced to an excited group of women, "they know you are coming."

She felt hopeful. She was going to see Herman again. There was no need to pack. Her backpack and her photo album were lost. By the time she kissed Gerdi and Emile goodbye, she was in a better mood. She was going to join Herman.

It was the middle of the night, when she and nine hundred and ninety nine other women boarded the train. She thought of her mother and father, and little Judie, wondering where they were, and when she would see them again. Were they all right? She dozed off.

The packed car had two buckets; one was filled with drinking water, the other was a toilet. But, the conditions were so squalid, that by drinking from the water bucket, you could as well have been drinking from the toilet bucket.

14. Auschwitz - Birkenau

Death camp Birkenau (also known as Auschwitz II) was situated four and a half miles northwest of Auschwitz I and was surrounded by ditches, guard posts, and 2000-volt barbed wire. Upon arrival, those too young and too old to work were ordered to undress in an area that resembled the changing room of a swimming pool; the spotless room included hooks with numbers. They were told to tie their shoelaces together and they were given soap and towels. There were signs that said, "Keep clean," "Don't forget your soap" and "Remember you hook number." Some 950 people were corralled into the "shower room." A thick steel door, just like the door of a bank vault, sealed the room airtight. An SS soldier climbed onto the roof and threw Zyclon-B cyanide gas capsules down through a skylight. When the capsules released the gas, the people in the chamber yelled, cried, and begged to be let out. It took half an hour before everyone was dead. Occasionally a child survived because an air bubble had formed beneath a pile of bodies. They were shot on the spot. Mouths were inspected for gold, which then was melted and deposited in Nazi bank accounts.

The infamous Dr. Josef Mengele

***

After seventy-two hours, the train finally jolted to a stop. They felt stiff and filthy. They were dehydrated and exhausted.

Outside, they heard dogs barking. The bolt outside was disengaged and the door slid open. Bright searchlights focused on the opening. Men were shouting instructions in Polish and German.

"*Raus, raus.*"

"Get off the train and leave your stuff in the train."

"Leave your luggage behind! Line up in rows of five! Leave all your belongings on the train!"

Sonja stood in the doorway and hesitated. The bright searchlights blinded her.

"Leave your luggage on the train."

A feel of gloom engulfed her. What was Herman doing here? Where is he? They promised.

"Surrender your watches and rings."

Armed guards pushed them into a line that moved steadily towards six or seven men sitting behind a table. One man was wearing a doctor's coat. With a snap of his finger, he sent thousands of people to die. It might well have been the infamous and ruthless Dr. Mengele, also known as the Angel of Death.

A woman ahead of Sonja in line turned and said, "They're asking if you are healthy and if you can work."

The doctor looked at a grandmother and her grand children and motioned them to a waiting truck to their left. The mother of the children was motioned to the right, and she asked if she could join her mother and her children.

"You'll see them tonight," he answered politely.

"See you later, Mom," she called after her mother. "Take good care of the children."

"I've worked hard enough in Theresienstadt. I want to save my energy. I don't want to work," said the woman in front of her to the doctor. The doctor put her at ease and assured her that she didn't have to work at all, if she didn't want to. He motioned her to the truck.

When her eyes adjusted, she saw the barbed wire, the barking dogs, and the men in striped black and white prison garb, yelling at the women. She noticed a woman behind barbed wire dressed in black rags and a dirty headscarf, holding her hands out in front of her.

"What does she want?" Sonja asked.

"She's Polish, she's asking for food," someone whispered. Again, the woman held her hands up.

"Food, food, please?" she cried in Polish. Suddenly, they heard a gunshot. The woman fell backward and Sonja saw that she wasn't wearing any underwear.

"Oh, my God, what is this place? This must be hell," she whispered.

It was Sonja's turn. She stepped forward and stood eye-to-eye with the doctor.

"Are you healthy?"

"Yes."

"Do you want to work?"

"Yes."

He sent her to the right.

Of the nearly thousand women on her transport, only fifty or sixty passed the selection. All the others were sent to die.

An hour later, most of the women that had come on the same train were dead. Gassed. Murdered.

Escorted by guards and barking dogs, Sonja's group walked into concentration camp Auschwitz. They were taken to an area and told to undress. It was freezing cold; they were filthy and looking forward to a hot shower.

A pregnant woman took off her coat and started to undress.

"What are you doing here?" A guard asked her politely, when he noticed she was pregnant. He called his young assistant.

"This young lady here is in the wrong place. Take her to where she belongs."

Her mother asked if she could go with her daughter.

"Yes, of course, you may." He smiled. The assistant took both of them to the gas chamber.

They used dull razors and did a quick and rough job, leaving cuts and traces of blood on all of them. Their head, their armpits, their legs, and their pubic areas were shaved. Next, they were taken to a shower room and told to wait. It was just a few drops of icy water, but it was water.

Naked and wet, they were rushed out of the shower and into to a barracks crammed with giant piles of used clothes, almost reaching the ceiling.

CaPo's kept yelling, "Take three pieces only and stand in line. Three pieces only and hurry!"

Sonja grabbed a torn, thin, summer dress and a flannel overall for underneath the dress. She snatched an old dirty coat with a cross stitched on its back. A woman who took an extra shirt got a beating and dropped the shirt. Sonja found two left shoes that were two sizes too small, but it's all she had time for.

By now, it was two o'clock in the morning. What are they going to do with us? I need to find Herman.

They were ordered to stand in rows of ten. All of a sudden, she was part of an enormous convoy comprised of one thousand women in one hundred rows of ten. Where did they all come from? It seemed unreal. Suddenly, she started itching really badly. Her clothes were full with fleas.

Guards watched from the towers as the one thousand powerless women were escorted out of the camp. It was two o'clock in the morning.

An hour later, they marched through the gates of Birkenau. The women were exhausted and discouraged. Searchlights illuminated endless rows of wooden barracks dissected by muddy walkways. There was a foul, pungent odor in the air that they couldn't place. A woman in the outside row asked a guard, "What is that smell?"

"That's the bakery," he laughed, knowing the smell came from the ovens burning the bodies of the people who were killed in the gas chambers.

His answer spread like wildfire amongst the women who happily believed there was a bakery on site.

Men and women were kept in separate areas. Female prisoners ran the female section. Just as in Westerbork and Theresienstadt, the most important jobs involved food and were mostly available through connections that were built over time.

The Polish CaPo's (Camp Police) were responsible for law and order. The most senior CaPo had a whip. She knew the SS guards wanted to see her use it, in return for extra food, she needed to be whipping somebody constantly, or they'd replace her.

The thousand women entered a wooden barracks and found themselves in an enormous warehouse-type space filled with about four hundred triple bunk beds. Three women shared a bed and instead of a mattress, they slept on jute bags filled with sand, gravel, and straw. It was so tight that when one of them turned, the other two had to turn too.

Birkenau Barracks, 1000 women

Toilets were in a separate building nearby and comprised two rows of twenty holes in the ground, non-partitioned. The stench was brutal, with feces everywhere. There was no toilet paper and everyone walked right through the mess; dysentery and typhoid claimed many lives.

There were two wood-burning stoves in the middle of the aisle. Small groups of Czech women that had arrived earlier stood around the stoves talking.

Roll call often lasted up to six hours during twenty degrees below zero. There was no talking. When women fainted, they fell in the snow, and froze to death. Their bodies were included in the count.

CaPo's handed out what looked like camping kits; aluminum dishes with a spoon and fork attached. The spoon was adorned with a tiny yet decorative swastika. If you lost your kit, you were out of luck. Every night, the barracks leader handed out "soup" with a small piece of bread. Soup was dirty water with shards of grass floating in it and caused many upset stomachs. Often unable to reach the toilets in time, they squatted wherever they were, even in their cage.

After dark, somewhere near the barbed wire behind her barracks, Sonja found a place where she went to the bathroom. She had no choice but to pull her pants up without wiping herself. She ate barely, and didn't need to go a whole lot. Her period had stopped due to a chemical the Germans added to the soup. Starvation and fear are also known to disrupt the cycle.

Sonja and her cousin Sere and a third woman shared a top bunk. There was incessant crying and screaming, but nobody paid attention. Sonja was overwhelmed by it all. She was so scared, that her stomach acted up, and she got the runs. Her cramps were agonizing. Afraid to leave, she took the clogs that Sere was using as a pillow but had slipped away from under her.

Careful not to wake her, she climbed down and defecated nervously, filling the first clog to the rim, than the second one. During roll call a few hours later, Sere stood barefoot on the freezing cobblestones. She cursed Sonja, who had confessed.

After a couple of days, she ventured out and found the washrooms. She looked at the two long rows of filthy basins with their thirty or so faucets that only dripped water. She decided it was safer not to wash.

She took a few small bites from her piece of bread and hid the left over piece under her mattress for later. When she wanted more bread, it was gone. Shocked, she did something she'd regret the rest of her life. She found someone else's piece and took it. Having stolen something was a shock. What would my father think of me now? An awful feeling came over her.

Then she saw him. At first, she wasn't sure it was him. He had lost weight. Jimmy waved as he came rushing her way.

"How are you? Where's Herman?"

"He's okay. I only have a second."

He quickly handed her a note. A few women from Holland gathered around him, as he confirmed a list of names he had memorized.

"You husbands want you to know they're okay and that they love you."

"My beautiful Sonja! If you get this note, I'll feel a whole lot better. Look up at the sky tonight. You'll see the moon. So will I. We're leaving tomorrow. Don't know where to. Jimmy turned out to be a good friend. America is going to take care of us. This will be over soon. I'll find you in Amsterdam. I promise. I love you." HR

She held on to his note, even while she ate and slept. She didn't let go until a few days later, when she woke up and saw her hand was empty. She searched everywhere but never found it. Sere thought someone had used it as toilet tissue. She was inconsolable, for a short while.

"Roll Call!" CaPo's shouted and blew their whistles at three-thirty am.

Those who climbed down from the bunks, hurried outside, into the November freeze. Those who didn't, were dead or dying. Their bodies were gone by the time the others returned. If it rained, they got wet to the bone. October had turned into November and by now, they looked unrecognizable.

Sometimes, they'd ask for volunteers in return for an extra piece of bread. Sonja and Sere speculated if they should or not. Sere volunteered one early morning.

With Sere gone, Sonja didn't want to stay in her bunk. She joined a few Czech women standing around the stove. They made conversation. She learned that they had arrived on the same train from Theresienstadt as she. They had families, husbands, lovers, and children. They asked about her and she told them about Herman. It was her longing for Herman, she told them that kept her going. They understood.

Sere returned that same evening. She had trouble walking.

"They made me wait the whole day, then all they did was take my blood. After the second bottle, I must have fainted. I came to outside in the snow. They must have thrown me out, just like that. It took an hour to find my way back. All these barracks look alike. I'm freezing."

Her whole body was sore. Sonja helped her up the bunk and kept her company. Later, when the soup was distributed, she made sure Sere got an extra serving.

Operating a gas chamber half-full was expensive. So, they held unexpected mini-selections in the middle of the night, looking for women to fill up the empty space in the chamber. They lined them up knee deep in the snow, and judged them in their nakedness.

You didn't want to stand next to someone looking heavier or healthier, because the sickest-looking were separated and trucked away into the heart of darkness and never seen again.

The gnawing hunger and the freezing weather kept many women from sleeping. Every so often, after they finally fell asleep, they were woken up.

"Get up, everybody!"

"Take off your clothes! Leave them inside!"

They were ordered to form a circle in a brightly lit open space. A doctor standing on a round drum stool had them run in circles around him. If he pointed his stick at you, you were to step out of the circle and get into the back of a waiting army truck. They were naked, terrified, and freezing. The weather was unbearable. Hands and feet that had thawed earlier now froze up again. Sonja's thumb had been throbbing since Theresienstadt, but trying to stay worm, she had ignored it. Reneetje from Holland was very thin. He pointed at her and a few others. Nobody ever saw them again. An hour or so later, Sonja and the others hobbled back to the barracks.

"We need a thousand women for a work detail outside the camp. Not too far from here," the head CaPo announced.

"I'll go mad if I stay here any longer."

All they could think of was getting away from the stinking odor and the fuming chimneys. They both volunteered.

It was dark, when one late afternoon, Sonja and Sere marched out of the barracks; Sonja was the corner person in the very last row of a thousand women. She could barely walk, but she didn't want to stay behind without Sere.

When they got to the gate, they were counted. Suddenly Sonja felt a burning pain.

"Thousand and one!" the CaPo barked.

"Back to your barracks!"

Panicked and confused, she was too scared to move. When she felt a second flogging, she turned around and started walking. All the barracks looked alike. She thought of Sere, who had trouble finding her way back in the daytime. Sere! She was gone. There'd been no time to say goodbye.

She waded through the mud, sinking to above her ankles. She tried to remember the way back, but she was completely lost. She was scared of being caught in the searchlights.

She encouraged herself, mumbling her father's words, "Everything happens for a reason."

She heard Herman's voice: "I'll find you, I promise." She looked up at the sky for the moon, but it was overcast. At the entrance of every barracks, she went up the two steps, opened the door, and looked for a familiar face. After fifteen or sixteen barracks, she finally recognized someone. She was cold and exhausted. Her thumb was hurting terribly. She looked at it and saw that she the nail was gone. Exhausted she closed her eyes.

"I'd never have survived that walk," she thought, back in her bunk.

Entrance Auschwitz Birkenau

cross against escape

female barracks

"sleeping quarters"

"toilets"

*Spoon and fork Sonja used in Auschwitz.
Note swastika imprint and year.*

roll call Birkenau

selection arrival Birkenau

15. Skin and Bones

At the beginning of 1945, the SS and the Wehrmacht (German army) were fighting over trains. The Wehrmacht needed trains to transport soldiers to the front; the SS needed trains to transport prisoners deeper into the Third Reich. With the allied armies approaching, the SS wanted to hide evidence of their crimes. All over Nazi Germany, prisoners were used as slave labor for the German war industry. In concentration camp Gross Rosen, they were put to work for Krupp, I.G. Farben, and Daimler Benz, the car company that makes Mercedes.

Original entrance Gross Rosen

***

There were about thirty or forty women left, three were from Holland. The following day, a new female transport arrived, and the barracks was filled to capacity yet again.

About ten days later, Sonja volunteered again. Her group was counted, everything was in order, but there was no train available. They stood motionless for what seemed forever, in the freezing weather and waited for a train.

A train finally arrived. They were exhausted, but relieved when the smoking chimneys disappeared on the horizon. She looked at the women around her, wrapped in filthy rags. They looked like skin and bones and smelled horribly. She had not looked in a mirror for months and wondered if she looked anything like them. *It's probably a good thing that Herman can't see me now.*

The train stopped in the city of Breslau, where they waited to transfer. Sonja sat next to the window. A young man on the platform saw the group of filthy prisoners and spat against her window. After several hours, a locomotive pulling open railcars arrived. They rode through woodlands and pastures, heading northwest to an outpost of Gross-Rosen concentration camp.

That winter of 1944 was unrelentingly cold. The wind-chill factor made it -32 degrees. They huddled together but not one of them was adequately dressed. Sonja's hands and toes were turning black from frostbite.

The train stopped in a forest just outside the tiny hamlet of Birnbäumel, which consisted of ten or so farms. When they finally got off the rail car, two women had frozen to death.

Nearly one thousand thin, unwashed, sickly-looking women walked knee-deep in snow, for about three-quarters of a mile into the forest. They arrived at a deserted camp.

The first thing she noticed was the absence of guard towers and barbed wire. There were no chimneys, and the unbearable stench was absent. Instead of a sadistic block leader, a friendly Hungarian CaPo lived with her family in a separate shed.

There were ten round horse stables. Since the horses were used to standing on firm ground, the wooden stables had no floorboards and the outside paneling stopped eight inches above the ground.

One hundred women were assigned to one stable. They shared twenty-five straw mattresses and a few old, dirty, torn up horse blankets. The mattresses were placed in a circle around a small stove in the center. There was no running water. They washed with snow.

The moment they arrived, they were handed shovels and ordered to fill up the eight-inch opening to stop the draft.

When that was done, they were famished, but it was six o'clock and time for roll call. An SS captain appeared.

"Is there a secretary in this group?"

Maybe mother was right after all and my typing skills will come in handy. If I get through this, I can follow a nursing…

Her thoughts were interrupted.

"Is there a secretary in this group?"

She stepped forward.

"I'm a secretary, Herr *Hauptsturmführer*."

He walked over to her.

"Show me your hands."

He saw her abscessed thumb with the nail missing and screamed at her.

"What are you thinking, you dirty, rotten Jewish swine?"

The first blow drove the air from her lungs. She lost her balance and fell to the snow. Enraged, he kicked her mercilessly.

When he was done with her, he walked away. She bled from her ears and mouth. Her upper teeth were dislodged. Two women helped her up.

A sergeant called out their names from a list and checked them off. When he was done, he looked at the miserable group in rags.

"You are not dressed for this kind of weather. I will try to get you clothing. If I don't succeed, I will have to send you back to Auschwitz."

They were dismissed and sent to their stables without food. Somebody overheard him tell his assistant, "If I don't get clothes for these bitches, I'll ship them back. I don't feel like burying a thousand corpses. Call Gross Rosen and tell them I need clothes."

Sonja and the Czech women slept in the same stable. Branches were piled near the entrance to keep the snow out. Sonja slept right next to the branches.

After the morning roll call, the women got two slices of moldy bread. Sonja ate both slices immediately. No more saving for later.

Guarded by SS soldiers wearing warm sweaters and thick, long warm winter coats, the women marched into the forest, carrying their shovels upside down against their shoulders.

A female guard goaded them, "Left, right, left, right." As they marched past the farms, they were ordered to sing popular Nazi songs. Two mothers watched. A few children stopped playing and started throwing stones at them.

"Dirty Jew women, dirty Jew women."

The mothers laughed.

"Dig!" they were ordered. "Dig, until you see water!"

The frozen ground made trench digging almost impossible, but once they got through the upper layer, it became easier.

They dug from six in the morning to six in the evening, knee-deep in the snow, while the warmly dressed guards talked and joked around a campfire.

The first day, around midday, a man and a woman riding a horse-drawn cart from a nearby farm, brought two big milk containers filled with food. Sonja's group got a dish with potatoes, meat, onions, and gravy. It had been eighteen months since they enjoyed a meal. It was incredible. One of the girls in Sonja's group said, "Quick, finish your food. This can't be for us."

When the next group was being fed, the guards noticed what was going on and came running up to the couple, cursing, and swearing. The following day, the couple showed again, but now for lunch they got soup; water with a few stalks of grass.

It was four o'clock in the morning; it was dark out and brutally cold.

"Get up! Roll call," the CaPo yelled. "Line up outside."

"I'm so cold, I'm going to die today," Sonja thought as she folded the blanket and placed it at the foot of the mattress for inspection.

Two hours later, the women grabbed their shovels and lined up. Sonja used the moment to grab the blanket from her mattress in the stable. While on her knees wrapping herself in the blanket, the door opened and a guard looked in. She didn't notice Sonja behind the pile of branches and left. Even with the blanket, she kept shivering. The following day, the sergeant warned them that the guards had noticed that blankets were missing.

"You are to leave the blankets in the stable."

Without barbed wire, the guard towers, the barking dogs, and the searchlights, the women started to feel a bit less fearful. Now and then, Sonja sang for them. Somebody would start singing, hoping she'd join in. The guards liked her voice too. Every so often, a guard checked their progress, and the women stopped singing and dug harder. When they returned to the camp, she didn't feel her hands and her toes anymore. It was dark by then and again time for roll call. After they were counted, they were handed two slices of stale bread and sent to bed. When Sonja saw a CaPo throw out rotten potato skins, she got permission to share them with the women in her stable. They didn't believe their luck.

Everybody suffered frostbite to some degree. Sonja's hands and feet were black, covered with infected wounds. Her nose felt also frozen. She could barely walk. At night, beneath the filthy blanket, her thawing body felt like torture. There was continuous moaning throughout the night. When she dozed off, it was time for roll call all over again. Every morning they found dead women.

A supply of soiled clothing had arrived. To everybody's surprise, Stella, one of the Dutch girls found her own coat that she had left in Auschwitz. The bonnet her mother had crocheted was still in the pocket. The CaPo allowed Stella to wear her own coat.

During a roll call, she looked at her thumb and told herself, "When I see the white crescent of a new nail, I must be free, or I'll give up. I can't go on like this."

She thought of Herman, her parents, Judie. She saw her dad in her mind, pushing a wheelbarrow in Westerbork.

At night, while trying to get warm, the girls asked her to sing. She imitated some famous singer and sang until she fell asleep.

On Christmas day, the CaPo told her that the guards wanted her to sing for them. Perhaps I should, so I can ask them for some bread for the girls and me, she thought. Nervously, Sonja followed the CaPo through the thick snow to the administration stable. Inside, it was nice and warm. Guards were celebrating with food and liquor. Her stomach ached from being hungry and all she could think of was the bread she was hoping to get.

"I'm here to sing," she told them shyly. They circled around her and requested a song. She tried a few notes, but she was too weak and too nervous and started to cry.

"I'm sorry, I can't," she apologized.

They saw her frostbitten fingers.

"Get out of here before you make us sick!"

She forgot to ask for bread. She entered the stable empty handed. The women were disappointed, but they understood.

"Just as well. It's not as if you really want to sing for those bastards."

Sonja's hands and feet were decomposing. Putrid chunks of flesh fell from her fingers. A few toes were hanging on by threads of skin. She kept pushing them back into place every so often.

"Keep going, or you'll be sent back to Auschwitz, and you know what that means."

Then the moment they'd been waiting for arrived. In the distance, they heard the sound of artillery fire.

16. The Beginning of the End

January 1945. The Soviets were headed towards Berlin. Reichsführer SS Heinrich Himmler ordered concentration camps to transport their prisoners to "safer" camps deeper into German territory. Hitler was still optimistic when he said, "The German leadership is determined to brave every crisis. The Third Reich will not be deterred; it will never capitulate."

Soviets hoisting Soviet flag in Berlin

***

One of the CaPo's had said that at any moment now, the war could be over. But Sonja didn't trust the rumor and at night, she dragged herself out of the stable and asked a guard.

"Go to sleep; it's almost over."

"This Friday, we will evacuate. Those of you who can walk must be ready to walk to Gross-Rosen. It'll take three days. Those of you who can't walk, report to the sick bay," a guard announced. They calculated the odds of walking three days, thirty-five miles a day, through the snow.

Sonja's hands and arms were black up to her elbows; her feet were frozen. She couldn't walk. She thought of Herman. She wanted to live so badly. Thinking of him had kept her going, but for how much longer?

Anxiously, one woman grabbed her arm. "You're not going to walk, are you?" She showed her feet.

"Even if I wanted to, I couldn't."

The woman rolled her eyes hysterically and started yelling, pulling at Sonja's arm. "If you stay, I stay."

Sonja calmed her down. She asked the other women what they planned on doing. They were afraid to stay behind.

They didn't stand a chance. They weren't dressed for it—no socks, no shoes. Only one woman survived the death march, as they were called. She managed to run into an empty house and hide. Similar death marches, all over Germany and Poland left thousands of dead bodies in their wake.

About sixty women remained behind, including the five Czech women whom Sonja had befriended. That night, they slept in the sick bay, as they were ordered.

January 27, 1945 fell on a Saturday morning. They were woken up at daybreak by distant artillery, but the camp was unusually quiet. No roll call? Someone opened the door and looked out. The sun was shining, but it was very cold, about -13 degrees.

"It looks like they're gone."

They waited an hour or so before some women left the sickbay to explore.

"They've taken all the food. We're going to explore some more."

They went to the farms to find out what was going on. Some of the women decided to remain there. Others returned with warm woolen sweaters and warm coats.

Only twenty now remained in the sick bay, of which Sonja was one. Nobody bothered with them.

She was thirsty, and eyed the icicles hanging from the slanted ceiling beams. She hoisted herself up, snapped a couple of icicles for the others, and kept one for herself. She lay down again and pretended to have won a lollipop.

Two days later, the door of the sickbay opened, and a Soviet soldier wearing a fur cap stuck his head in. When he saw the emaciated women, he got on his knees and said "Gleb."

"We will bring you bread." He backed out and called his mates. Two others looked in. A little later, they brought bread to last for a couple of days. Every couple of days a different friendly Red army soldier looked in on them.

The sound of heavy artillery in the surrounding area came closer. The Soviets brought them food every day. Three weeks later, when her feet had improved somewhat, she tried to find a warm place to sleep. They were told to be careful, because there were still plenty of Germans in the area.

She dragged herself to the nearest farmhouse and knocked on the door. There was no answer. The door was unlocked and she entered. She met a woman in the hallway who carried a delicious smelling cake, straight out of the oven.

"Please, may I sleep here?"

The woman ignored her and continued down the hall. She entered the family room and before she closed the door Sonja heard her say in German, "There's a filthy woman from the camp in the hallway."

Frightened she continued down to the next farm. A forester, with a feather in his green cap allowed her to stay.

She wanted to wash herself, but she was afraid to undress. For the first time in years, she slept on a bed with a mattress. There were no sheets, but there were blankets.

In the morning, she dragged herself from the farm back to the camp. There, she listened to the latest rumors and ate the food the Soviets brought every couple of days. They warned her to be careful about eating. Her body had to be reacquainted with solid foods. Many prisoners had died from eating too much, too fast. In the evening, she went back to the farmhouse.

At four in the morning, she woke up with an upset stomach and used a bucket. When she was done, she wanted to go outside to empty the bucket in the woods.

The bedroom door creaked when she opened it. The light at the end of the hallway in the kitchen was on and she heard two voices whisper in German.

"Who's there?"

"There's a woman from the camp sleeping here." She recognized the forester's voice.

She stayed still and listened.

"Don't worry. The Führer has developed a new weapon. Our boys will be back in a few days and finish the job. We are going to win this war."

She heard them laugh.

Too scared to empty the bucket and too scared to go back to bed, she sat down on the floor against the door and waited for the morning.

The next couple of nights, Sonja found a mattress in the stable where the guards had lived. At night, the stable was filled with people and rats, both looking for a warm place to spend the night.

Throughout the night, something touching her feet kept waking her. Thinking it was a rat she moved her foot. She was too exhausted to bother. After a couple of times, she made a mental note to tell someone about the rat in the morning.

In the morning, the arm of a dead woman was touching her foot. The woman had tried to ask her for help. Sonja felt awful and the guilt for not helping her stayed with her the rest of her life.

Twenty-four hours later, Soviet trucks arrived and took them to the city of Trachenberg, which was under Soviet control. It was another three or four weeks before the Soviets had liberated the whole area.

17. Undetermined

The allied forces comprised of many countries. North African soldiers from Morocco, Algiers, and Tunisia, and Canadian, New Zealand and Australian soldiers, the United States and the Soviet Union, all fought Nazi Germany and helped liberate Europe.

***

Amsterdam 1945. The five-year Nazi occupation had ended. The war was over. After getting back to Amsterdam, she gathered herself and began to rebuild. She heard that the People's Reparation Office was looking for a typist. She applied and was hired. Her job was to register the returning Jews; who was dead, who was alive, where had they been, etc. The job was taxing. All day she'd listen to survivors and their accounts. Every story was different, yet similar. That was no consolation. Hoping it would help her recover it only deepened an already open wound.

Stacked file cabinets lined the walls with drawers too stuffed to close. Sonja sat at her desk. Her eyes were fixed on two registration cards with her parents' names on it. Her boss saw she was restless.

"Go and take your lunch break. Just be back on time," said her boss kindly.

Sonja jumped on her bike and hurried to Central Station. There were many soldiers about. Buildings were damaged, streets were broken up, and there was rubble everywhere. Store windows were shattered; some were boarded shut.

Out of breath, she found a spot to park her bike. It was busy. Trains were coming and going. People were returning from the war, many happily reuniting.

She positioned herself next to a big handwritten sign that said FREE COFFEE. Then she saw them. They looked weathered and exhausted, with no luggage. Not long ago, she'd arrived just like them. She went up to them and asked if they knew Herman Rosenstein.

Three times a day she waited, but so far no sign of Herman. She kept hoping against hope. Her mom and dad and her sister were dead, but not Herman. He couldn't be.

"Tomorrow's another day," her boss encouraged her back at the office.

She pushed her bike into the neglected garden and leaned it against the scruffy hedge. The hedge gave way and it took an effort not to crash with bike and all into their neighbor's garden. She repositioned the bike.

Her mind wandered back in time as she climbed the steps to the front door. Over there was the room where Herman had asked her dad for permission to marry. I would be easier for him to protect Sonja and the family as his son in law, he'd explained. Her dad and her mom had started to take a liking to Herman.

Her parents and her little sister, she thought for the hundredth time that day, were dead. She would never see them again. She closed the front door and cried. How can they all be gone?

She took two the registration cards from her purse. Her eyes were on the date in red pencil 29-6-43 and the word DEPORTED written diagonally over her parents' names. She cried.

"Sonja, is that you?"

A door opened. Cousin Judy noticed the cards in Sonja's hand. "What are those?"

"My parents' registration cards. I didn't want them in the drawer with the people that are confirmed dead."

Emotionally she continued, "I forgot my sister's card."

Cousin Judy hugged her. "Come on, have a cup of tea with us."

Anton's wife Jet was as thin as a rake. She and her daughter, cousin Judy, were drinking tea.

The few pieces of furniture in the living room were second-hand. The house uncle Anton had lived before the war had been condemned. From the ground up, all the way through the roof, you could see the sky.

All wood had been gutted and used as firewood during the cold winter of 1944. The central heating system had been stolen, and their personal belongings were gone.

Cousin Judy had managed to get a house assigned to her parents so that Anton could resume his medical practice.

Jet mentioned that she'd visited their former neighbor who had offered to safe keep Anton's paintings. Jet asked him if she could please them back.

"Those paintings," the neighbor had answered, "have been hanging on my wall for years."

There were plenty of similar stories going around. Jet didn't bother with the paintings. But there was no denying that the curtains he had also kept, matched their wallpaper. The older homes had old-fashioned high ceilings, and so the curtains were long and heavy. Carrying them was almost impossible. Sonja put them over her shoulders like a long veil and dragged them to the their new address, half a block away.

She didn't tell anybody about her going to the station every day, where she waited for Herman. It was all she could think of. She did not want to live without him. He was her everything, her reason for making it through. Her love for him had given her hope. She survived for Herman.

While they speculated who was still alive and who wasn't, Sonja thought of Herman. Was he coming back? Why wasn't he back yet?

His registration card said 'undetermined.' She burst into tears when she thought of his note she'd lost. Life was senseless without him and not worth living. She got up and ran out of the room. Judy told them about the registration cards.

She lay down on her bed and let her tears flow freely. She sobbed. No, she told herself again, she didn't want to live without Herman. Through her tears, she looked at a bunch of dried carnations on the wall, his bride's bouquet to her.

She heard his voice; I will love you as long as I live. Her thoughts went back to that very last moment in Theresienstadt, before he had turned around and walked away. She took her pillow, placed it on her mouth, and screamed.

Exhausted her mind took her back to the moment where there was ample reason to believe that Herman was alive.

18. Displaced Persons

While the south of Holland had been liberated in September of 1944, it would take until May of 1945 for the whole country to be free, and for the war in Holland to be officially over. The Americans liberated concentration camp Buchenwald, the Soviets went on to liberate Vienna, and the British liberated the notorious concentration camp of Bergen-Belsen and the Soviets liberated Prague. Heavy fighting continued in the surrounding area.

***

A friendly Soviet doctor treated her hands and her feet. She washed for the first time in months. She had a feeling that her parents were not alive anymore. But Herman? Herman would come back.

Trains were leaving for Western Europe, but armies were still fighting and for months, they traveled through the snow-covered Carpathian Mountains, back and forth between Poland and Czechoslovakia. She was asked and assisted taking care of the wounded soldiers.

"Why don't we go to Prague on our own?" said one of the Czech women after a few weeks.

"This is taking too long."

They liked the idea and Sonja decided to join them. They took a train towards the Czech border and walked for two days, until they reached the border. Her Czech friends told her to keep quiet while crossing. It turned out to be good advice. Once across, they continued walking. They wanted to get to Kosice.

They walked for days, through stunning forests and picturesque mountains. Farmers provided them with bread and allowed them to sleep in the stables. It slowly started to sink in that they were free. The fresh air and the beautiful scenery were marred by evidence of the war. Even after her Auschwitz experience of hunger, fear, and pain, the dead body of a horse and its rider upset her deeply.

On a Friday at sundown, they met a couple on their way to a synagogue.

"Where have you girls been?"

"Auschwitz."

"That must have been terrible. Where are you headed now?"

"We are taking Sonja to Kosice, and we'll go on to Prague."

"My name is Mathilde," said the woman.

"My sister Malvine lives in Kosice."

Mathilde scribbled a note, handed it to Sonja, and told her to go and see her sister.

They walked for two more weeks when they finally arrived in Kosice. At the community center, they said tearful goodbyes.

While waiting for assistance, Sonja fainted and woke up in a hospital. She complained about her body itching all over. They ran her bath. As soon as she got into the tub, the water became alive with fleas. She hadn't washed properly in so long, that by the time the tub was filled, the water had turned black.

They fed her and put her in a clean bed. She slept for seventy hours straight. When she woke up, she remembered the note for Malvine and gave it to the nurse.

Three days later, Malvine and her eight-year-old son paid her a visit. The hospital was short on beds, and after she made more progress, Malvine was allowed to take Sonja home with her where she could rest.

Malvine gave her some of her clothes and her husband, a shoemaker whose clients included the Czech president, gave her a pair of shoes. They took wonderful care of her. Malvine was a great cook, and Sonja was gaining weight. She could not have met nicer people.

Some weeks later, the Soviets announced that in cooperation with the allied countries of origin, they were preparing the journey home for all displaced persons (DPs).

The DPs in Kosice and surroundings, mostly Germans, French, Belgians, and a small number were Dutch, were called to report to the Soviet embassy.

When Sonja went to make inquiries, they kept her there with thousands of other DPs from Western Europe.

Malvine heard about it, and brought her a delicious cake.

The Soviets made them watch movies showing what the Nazis had done in Poland and Russia. They saw how adults and children were forced into a church, which was then set on fire, with everybody inside burning to death. They saw pictures of gas chambers, crematoria, and lampshades made of human skin.

Only now did it sink in, that she might never see her parents or sister again. She recalled how her mother had her feet operation, to improve her walking. Could they have survived Sobibor?

A train left for Pilzen, a city in western Czechoslovakia. It was packed with grateful survivors. The weather was getting better and they traveled on the roof in awe of an expansive landscape.

In Pilzen, they saw chickens and geese for the first time.

Someone yelled ecstatically, "That must be the Americans."

The Soviets handed them over to the Americans, who gave them chocolate and eggs. Then there was more good news. France was liberated.

19. Home

The Allied countries sent trains and airplanes to bring their nationals home. Sonja and the other Dutch survivors waited in anticipation. They waited and waited and waited. Not a word from the Dutch government. No telegram, no plane, or train to pick up them up.

At the beginning of June, while she was heating porridge, a Belgian government-sponsored DC-3 airplane landed to pick up its nationals. She and the other Dutch survivors were allowed to catch a ride to the city of Brussels. The interior of the plane was gutted and fitted with benches along the walls. If the Belgian government had not sent an airplane, would she still be waiting in Pilzen? She often wondered who turned off the gas and ate the porridge.

***

She was in Brussels and she was free, but she wanted to go home. The bus and train services hadn't started up yet. A horrible feeling about her mom and dad took hold of her. Herman made it through, for sure, perhaps her sister Judie too. It would be another couple of weeks before she could travel north.

As if time had stopped, the local theater was still showing *The Immortal Waltz*. It had been the last movie Sonja, her mom, and her sister enjoyed together. It felt surreal, as if the war had never happened.

The Belgians were considerate and hospitable to the returning DPs; the Salvation Army housed and fed them. Movie theaters, and bus services were free of charge to them. They were easily recognized; many still wore their striped camp pajamas.

It was a different story at the Dutch consulate in Brussels. The consul needed a secretary. Sonja had no money and was eager to work. She reported to the Dutch consulate. After being hired, she asked her new boss, for reading glasses. Hers were taken away from her in Auschwitz.

The consul lost it.

"How dare you? Go to Holland and see for yourself. Holland is a poor country. There's no money for eyeglasses."

She finally hitched a ride and continued to Den Bosch, the town where she was born only twenty-two years earlier. She visited her mother's domestic help, who had explained to her about the storks and the babies.

Marietje welcomed her warmly.

"They have taken the whole family. I heard they're all dead."

Marietje's husband had never liked Sonja and Judie. He complained that Marietje doted on them excessively. When he came home, he said to Sonja, "Well, well, you're back."

"Wouter, stop it," Marietje reproached him. "Think of everything she's endured."

"It's her own fault. They killed our lord Jesus," he shot back scornfully.

She continued on a barge to the city of Rotterdam. From there, she took the train to Amsterdam Central Station. Home at last. Maybe Herman got back before her?

20. Young legs

In 2010, a prominent Dutch politician sparked a heated debate in the Netherlands by saying that practicing Jews had "no future here, and should emigrate to the U.S. or Israel."

A friend of the Dutch queen recently told a Dutch newspaper that she was "almost proud to be called anti-Semitic."

Perhaps, that attitude is why it happened in Holland.

***

It was one o'clock in the morning, when she arrived at Amsterdam's Central Station, in the midst of worn-out soldiers, returning slave laborers and camp survivors. She was penniless.

She was back, but she wasn't she feeling great at all. An ominous feeling had taken hold of her.

She noticed a table with cups of coffee and a large sign that read FREE COFFEE. A few in her group went over there. The station manager charged toward them.

"Hands off!" he barked.

"Coffee is for soldiers returning from the front only."

He pointed them towards Red Cross personnel sitting behind a table.

Indifferently, the woman behind the table registered her as "returned alive." She rattled off a list of questions.

"Name? Where have you been?"

Lastly, she asked matter-of-factly whether Sonja knew of any other survivors. She answered that she has a gut feeling her parents and her little sister had not survived Sobibor.

She glanced at the clock.

When the woman had finished filling out Sonja's forms, she explained that the Portuguese hospital was being used as a shelter.

"You can go and sleep there, here's a voucher."

"How do I get there? It is a long way from here."

The woman looked demonstratively at her legs.

"You've got young legs. A walk won't kill you. Do you have any luggage?"

"No, no luggage. Not a dime, not a penny."

At half-past one, she started the long walk to the shelter.

21. Where is Herman?

Once the survivors returned home, they searched for family and friends, mostly in vain, and for personal belongings they had given to friends and neighbors for safekeeping. Often the safe keepers refused to return the belongings or they had sold them.

***

May 1945. The war was over. Entire families were gone. The country was celebrating, not Sonja. She needed to find Herman.

For the survivors, the misery was about to start all over again. Who was alive and who was dead? Who was returning, and who was not?

Early the following morning, she found her cousin Judy. They hugged it seemed for hours.

"Everybody's dead!" Sonja blurted out finally.

She couldn't hold it in any longer.

"Nobody is coming back!"

"My parents are alive. They were in camp Bergen Belsen," Judy answered. On the train home, Sonja had heard stories about Bergen-Belsen.

"Impossible."

Sonja couldn't understand how Anton and Jet had survived Bergen-Belsen. But, a few weeks later, they too were back in Amsterdam. They stayed with friends until they got a residence assigned.

Sonja knew that her mother had given the neighbors and her domestic help personal belongings and valuables for safekeeping. With the most outrageous excuses, many safe-keepers claimed they'd been gifts. And a gift was a gift. When Anton went to pick up his car, his friend demanded thousands of guilders for, as he called it, a parking fee.

Her knees were shaking as she rang the doorbell. Mrs. Roderigues opened the door and turned white. They hugged.

"Are father and mother alive?"

"I don't know yet."

Mrs. Roderigues pulled her inside. They drank a cup of tea in the kitchen and she asked Sonja to tell her what happened. When Sonja was finished, Mrs. Roderigues got up.

She spread a newspaper on the kitchen table. Next, she got a few potted plants from the windowsill and turned the pots upside down. She was careful to empty the soil onto the newspaper.

From the soil appeared several aspirin vials containing her mom's jewelry and dad's pocket watch. She explained that the police had come by a few times and searched the house, but they never found a thing. She got up again and returned with Sonja's wedding dress, silver dinner utensils, some of Judie's clothes, Judie's camera, and a bunch of dried carnations. Lastly, she handed her an opened package of tea, apologizing for having opened it.

"There was no tea anywhere, but," she promised, "as soon as I get tea coupons, I'll give you a new package."

Gratefully, Sonja gave her the camera and the clothes for her two children. The neighbor had rescued some of her books. He returned all of them, including *The Clog Maker and the Princess*. She cried when she saw the book. She cried a lot these days.

When she went to pick up the bikes, the storeowner recognized her, and she knew something was wrong.

"I sold them, but as soon as new ones are available, you will get two brand new bikes from me.

Meanwhile," he suggested, "use this old bike, if you like."

She looked at the old, rickety bike. She thanked him and rode off in tears.

Three times a day, before work, during her lunch hour and after work, she went to the station and waited for Herman. Every day, she'd leave without him. Leaving for the third time that day, she rode to the shelter. Survivors were still arriving. Perhaps she'd missed him.

What if? How was she going to cope without him? She thought of the letter that had recently arrived from America. The paperwork had been approved. A relative of his had invited them. I am going to wait for Herman. We will go to America together, she thought as she parked her bike.

For no reason at all, she looked up and saw a familiar face quickly pulling back from the open window.

"Jimmy?" she screamed.

She relived her treasured last moments with Herman in Theresienstadt. Jimmy had walked ahead to the train.

"I'll find you." Herman had promised. They'd kissed and had promised that everything was going to be fine. She had so wanted to believe him.

"Jimmy!" she screamed, as she ran up the stairs.

"Jimmy! You're back," she cried.

Jimmy met her in the hallway.

"Where is Herman?" she asked frantically.

Jimmy hesitated, looking for words.

"Jimmy, please, I need to know. Where's Herman?" she screamed. Jimmy grabbed a nearby chair and sat her down.

A long pause.

"Sonja, Herman is dead."

"We were in the train, when Allied bombers started shooting at us. The train stopped, and while bombs struck all around us, we were ordered to get out and into the ditch. We left Herman and a few others in the train. They were too weak to move. When we got back, the train was destroyed and they were dead. We were told to leave their bodies in the ditch. I'm so sorry."

Sonja turned around, ran down the stairs, jumped on her bike, and took off. Dazed she arrived at the house where Mr. and Mrs. Gans were staying temporarily.

"Herman's dead!" she screamed, gutted by grief.

Mrs. Gans had treated Herman as her own son, even though quietly she'd been hoping that one day, Sonja would become her daughter-in-law by marrying her son Hansfried.

"He's not coming back!" she screamed. Mrs. Gans tried to calm her, but she was inconsolable.

She jumped up, ran out the door, and raced on her bike to Anton and Jet, where she collapsed. They carried her to the couch.

The doorbell rang and she heard Mrs. Gans's voice. Then everything went black. Hours later, she opened her eyes.

Uncle Anton sat by her side.

"You've cried yourself into a stupor."

He said calmly.

"You will come and live with us."

She deteriorated visibly. She lost interest, stayed indoors for many weeks.

Only five years earlier, she had been in school, living with her parents, dreaming about a future with Herman. Nearly all of the teachers and all her friends from school were dead.

In the Dutch language the word *vroeger,* roughly translates as "prior, " "earlier," or "before." For the Jews, it came to mean "before the war, when everybody was still alive."

DE DEPORTATIETRANSPORTEN

Datum	Transport	Bestemming		Datum	Transport	Bestemming
15 juli	1942-1137	personen naar Auschwitz		10 maart	1943-1105	personen naar Sobibor
16 juli	1942- 586	personen naar Auschwitz		17 maart	1943- 964	personen naar Sobibor
21 juli	1942-1002	personen naar Auschwitz		23 maart	1943-1250	personen naar Sobibor
24 juli	1942-1000	personen naar Auschwitz		30 maart	1943-1255	personen naar Sobibor
27 juli	1942-1010	personen naar Auschwitz		6 april	1943-2020	personen naar Sobibor
31 juli	1942-1007	personen naar Auschwitz		13 april	1943-1204	personen naar Sobibor
3 augustus	1942-1013	personen naar Auschwitz		20 april	1943-1166	personen naar Sobibor
7 augustus	1942- 989	personen naar Auschwitz		27 april	1943-1204	personen naar Sobibor
10 augustus	1942- 547	personen naar Auschwitz			- 196	personen naar Theresienstadt
14 augustus	1942- 505	personen naar Auschwitz		4 mei	1943-1187	personen naar Sobibor
17 augustus	1942- 510	personen naar Auschwitz		11 mei	1943-1446	personen naar Sobibor
21 augustus	1942-1003	personen naar Auschwitz		18 mei	1943-2511	personen naar Sobibor
24 augustus	1942- 551	personen naar Auschwitz		25 mei	1943-2862	personen naar Sobibor
28 augustus	1942- 608	personen naar Auschwitz		1 juni	1943-3006	personen naar Sobibor
31 augustus	1942- 560	personen naar Auschwitz		8 juni	1943-3017	personen naar Sobibor
4 september	1942- 714	personen naar Auschwitz		29 juni	1943-2397	personen naar Sobibor
7 september	1942- 930	personen naar Auschwitz		6 juli	1943-2417	personen naar Sobibor
11 september	1942- 874	personen naar Auschwitz		13 juli	1943-1988	personen naar Sobibor
14 september	1942- 902	personen naar Auschwitz		20 juli	1943-2209	personen naar Sobibor
18 september	1942-1004	personen naar Auschwitz		24 augustus	1943-1001	personen naar Auschwitz
21 september	1942- 713	personen naar Auschwitz		31 augustus	1943-1004	personen naar Auschwitz
25 september	1942- 928	personen naar Auschwitz		7 september	1943- 987	personen naar Auschwitz
28 september	1942- 610	personen naar Auschwitz		14 september	1943-1005	personen naar Auschwitz
2 oktober	1942-1014	personen naar Auschwitz			1943- 305	personen naar Theresienstadt
5 oktober	1942-2012	personen naar Auschwitz		21 september	1943- 979	personen naar Auschwitz
9 oktober	1942-1703	personen naar Auschwitz		19 oktober	1943-1007	personen naar Auschwitz
12 oktober	1942-1711	personen naar Auschwitz		16 november	1943- 995	personen naar Auschwitz
16 oktober	1942-1710	personen naar Auschwitz				
19 oktober	1942-1327	personen naar Auschwitz		11 januari	1944-1037	personen naar Bergen-Belsen
23 oktober	1942- 988	personen naar Auschwitz		18 januari	1944- 870	personen naar Theresienstadt
26 oktober	1942- 841	personen naar Auschwitz		25 januari	1944- 949	personen naar Auschwitz
30 oktober	1942- 659	personen naar Auschwitz		1 februari	1944- 908	personen naar Bergen-Belsen
2 november	1942- 954	personen naar Auschwitz		8 februari	1944-1015	personen naar Auschwitz
6 november	1942- 465	personen naar Auschwitz		15 februari	1944- 773	personen naar Bergen-Belsen
10 november	1942- 758	personen naar Auschwitz		25 februari	1944- 811	personen naar Theresienstadt
16 november	1942- 761	personen naar Auschwitz		3 maart	1944- 732	personen naar Auschwitz
20 november	1942- 726	personen naar Auschwitz		15 maart	1944- 210	personen naar Bergen Belsen
24 november	1942- 709	personen naar Auschwitz		23 maart	1944- 599	personen naar Auschwitz
30 november	1942 826	personen naar Auschwitz		5 april	1944- 289	personen naar Theresienstadt
4 december	1942- 812	personen naar Auschwitz			1944- 240	personen naar Auschwitz
8 december	1942- 927	personen naar Auschwitz			1944- 101	personen naar Bergen-Belsen
12 december	1942- 757	personen naar Auschwitz		19 mei	1944- 453	personen naar Auschwitz
					1944- 238	personen naar Bergen-Belsen
11 januari	1943- 750	personen naar Auschwitz		3 juni	1944- 496	personen naar Auschwitz
18 januari	1943- 748	personen naar Auschwitz		31 juli	1944- 213	personen naar Theresienstadt
23 januari	1943- 516	personen naar Auschwitz			1944- 178	personen naar Bergen-Belsen
29 januari	1943- 659	personen naar Auschwitz		3 september	1944-1019	personen naar Auschwitz
2 februari	1943- 890	personen naar Auschwitz		4 september	1944-2087	personen naar Theresienstadt
9 februari	1943-1184	personen naar Auschwitz		13 september	1944- 279	personen naar Bergen-Belsen
16 februari	1943-1108	personen naar Auschwitz				
23 februari	1943-1101	personen naar Auschwitz				
2 maart	1943-1105	personen naar Sobibor				

✓ Jacob, Henriëtta en/and kleine Judie (little)

✓✓ Sonja en/and Herman

Deportation Transport list showing dates, number of persons, and which camp they were sent.

Yearly return visit to Auschwitz Birkenau,
Sonja (3rd from left) 1980's

AFSCHEIDS SYNDROOM - SEPARATION ANXIETY

Sonja, 2007

Sonja lives to see her story published

For more images please visit the website
www.neversurrender.me

22. Epilogue

When taking off from Amsterdam Airport, and watching the Dutch coastline disappear beneath the clouds below, I am reminded of the people who in 1940 so desperately tried to reach England.

I am grateful to simply sit in an airplane, warm and dry. When I land in Los Angeles, I am grateful for being let into the United States of America, without having to navigate on all fours through a hole in the fence in the middle of the night.

I hope my mother's story will inspire you when you find yourself hopeless. Upon reading this, I hope you realize the truth of what has happened. Be thankful and grateful for what you have and remember to never surrender.

--

23. Questions & Answers

"Mother, how did you survive?"
"By trying to remain inconspicuous."
*

I dreamed that my mother and I were hiding in a church. My mother wanted to pray. I heard footsteps and quickly called out to her, "Mother, quickly; we've got to hide."

**

"What attracted you to Herman?"
"He was funny and smart. We laughed a lot. He was crazy about me. He made me feel safe."
*

I looked at the only two photos saved of Herman.

**

"Did you miss Herman during your summer breaks in Zandvoort?"
"We wrote each other all the time and I came up with excuses why I had to go home to Amsterdam. But my mother saw right through me."
*

I was visiting with my mother. Jetlagged, I relaxed on the couch. Using special magnifying reading glasses, she was engrossed in Elie Wiesel's Night. I was reading about a man who had walked out of a concentration camp. He worked in an agriculture detail outside of camp Westerbork. He told the guard, that nature called and got permission, to do his business behind a tree. When he was done, he kept walking. He simply walked away. What a great story. There was no need to speak. We were busy with her war, 24-7, day and night.

**

"Mother, do you know the story of that German girl who was mad at her Jewish best friend? One day in 1941, the

German girl saw her Jewish friend with her parents waiting on the street corner at night, with their suitcases and their backpacks ready. They were being deported. They are moving, thought the German girl, not realizing what was really happening. She was angry and disappointed because her best friend had not even told her. Worse, she had not said good-bye. The following day, movers emptied her best friend's house. They took the furniture, the books, and the piano on which they had played together for many years."

*

Every time I've tried reading *Mein Kampf.* I've wanted to ask him what was it that made him so mad. How can you hate so many people, that you want them all dead? No wonder he suffered stomach pains, headaches, nausea, double vision, dizziness, tinnitus, and more. His hate tore him up.

**

"Mother, it sounds like you weren't busy with politics or trying to understand what was about to happen."
"All I could think of was Herman. Don't forget, you didn't know what was going to happen. No one knew. Of course, in hindsight looking back it's a different story."

*

The sun was setting on the horizon. The back cover of the book I was reading showed a photo of a huge Dutch Nazi rally in Amsterdam with everyone holding a swastika flag. I looked up and saw the sun disappear into the ocean. A feeling of intense gratefulness overwhelmed me.

**

"Did you ever try and persuade Herman to pack up and leave the country with you?"
"How could we leave? We had no money and where could we go? Herman told me not to worry. Besides, the first couple of months nothing changed."

*

111

Studying my mother's story lead me to study the politics of
Holland during World War II. This led me to the politics of
Germany, which led me to Hitler, Himmler, Eichmann, Göring,
Göbbels, Heydrich, Frank, Churchill, and Stalin. From there, I
moved on to study the history of concentration camps
Westerbork, Theresienstadt, and Auschwitz. Going further back
took me to World War I and Napoleon.

**

*"Mother, weren't you scared when the police put you on a
train and sent you on your way?"*
*"I thought I am young and strong. I thought I could work,
and I felt lucky for going to Herman."*
*

To prevent her story from gradually being forgotten, I felt
the urgency to document my mom's story now more than ever.
**
*"Mother, what kept you alive, while everyone around you
was dying?"*
*"Hope and wanting to be reunited with Herman and with
my parents so, all said and done, I think it was love."*
*

The more I learned about my mom's story, the more I
wanted to understand what had happened. I became obsessed,
engrossed, like a tiger that won't let go of its prey.

**

*We had a backpack ready because they could be coming for
us at any moment. We thought we had to work. That is what
they told us. We believed it. Do you understand they call Jews
smart? We weren't very smart, were we?"*

*

I dreamed that I wore a thin summer dress. I was hiding
somewhere in a building. Someone had given me a gun and I
had to get out of the building. When the door shut, I could not
get out, yet I managed to escape. I carried the gun with me. I

wanted to hide it, but did not know where. My dress had no pockets. I wanted to get rid of it. I was scared. There were cops everywhere. One stopped me. "Where did you get the gun?"

"I found it."

"Sure you did. Please, come with me."

I woke up with a jolt.

**

"Mother, I was born on a Tuesday."

"Yes, you were. Me, too."

"The trains left from Westerbork to Poland on Tuesdays. Tuesdays are my lucky days, which is freaky when so many people were sent to die on a Tuesday.

*

I dreamed that I was in a hurry. I had a plane to catch. There were all kinds of obstacles in my way.

I was traveling with a bicycle, a suitcase, and my back ball, which I had left at an Italian restaurant. They would not let me leave the restaurant. I told them that I had a plane to catch, and that they had to let me go. I woke up with a jolt.

**

"Do you feel guilty that you couldn't help your parents and your sister?"

"How could I have helped them? No one expected to happen what happened."

*

Reading about people starving changed my relationship with food. I went to the market, full of colorful fruits and vegetables. I could only stand in awe and silently take in the scene. If only we could share more. Every time I open the fridge door or step inside a supermarket, I think of all those people in the world who go hungry, and that there is not much we can do about it. I feel bad, especially for the children.

**

"Mother, how did you know that you didn't want to go to Auschwitz?"

"I didn't. We didn't know what Auschwitz was. I asked Uncle Feli in Westerbork, 'I heard that they kill people in Auschwitz?' He said, 'Oh, child, that is all nonsense, all propaganda.'

We felt that things were not good. But we didn't know what exactly."

*

Every time I pick up my mail, I remember that all it took was a note in the mail with instructions where, when and what time to report. The note instructed to leave 'live possessions' meaning dogs and cats behind.

**

"Mother, how do you feel when you hear someone deny the Holocaust?"

"They say that because they didn't go through it. In a way, you can't blame them. Our brains are too small to understand. We didn't understand it either."

*

Incredible. It would've been so easy to surrender to hate.
She harbors no hate. Even when she was in the middle of it, she never surrendered.

**

"Mother, did you ever think that only ten years later, you might be back with a new husband, four children, making dinner and doing laundry and life was normal again?"

"Never. Life was never normal again. On the outside, it may have seemed that way perhaps. I couldn't just move on and pretend it never happened."

**

"Mother, I would love to wake you up every day and prepare you a nice breakfast. But the best I can do is visit you a couple of months a year."

*

Only now do I understand that she did try to move on. She started a family, and subconsciously tried to leave it behind, only IT never left her.

**

"Mother, what do you think about the Polish government giving a permit to a nightclub right at the entrance of the Auschwitz camp?"

"They don't understand. We didn't understand."

*

I dream the same dream over and over again; I walk next to my mother up a steep hill. We are both dressed in filthy rags and we're dead tired. A few children run our way. They are laughing at us.

**

"Mother, what was your very first morning like, when you woke up in Westerbork? Did you think, 'Where am I?'

"I was relieved and happy to be near Herman. I did not have to be afraid anymore. We felt lucky that we were still in Holland. It never occurred to me they were going to separate us."

"What was it like waking up in Birkenau?"

"That was a catastrophe. I was in hell. I never saw Herman again.

"Did you doubt that you would see him again?"

"No, of course not."

"What about your parents and your sister? Where did you think they had gone?"

"There were rumors, but gas chambers? It just did not make any sense. It was a new concept that went right over my head."

*

I am on my stationary bike, reading in the paper an article on the war in Kosovo. I check the counter: 19 minutes and 40 seconds, 1941, 1942, 1943, 1944, 1945. Just numbers.

**

"Mother, you say 'how can I believe in God after everything I have experienced?' I asked a rabbi how I should answer you. He said, 'The fact that your mother survived is a miracle, a miracle of God.'"
Do you agree?"

*

What is our problem? We are programmed to forget so we can get on with it, but then it happens again. Yesterday's enemies are today's friends and tomorrow's enemies. I'm having a hard time wrapping my mind around it.

**

"Mother, who do feel hatred for Germans?"
"This is a new generation. Children and grandchildren are not responsible for their parents and grandparents actions. Germany has shown remorse."

*

North American Indians believe that God is present everywhere—in plants, in animals, in rivers, in every blade of grass, even in rocks. That philosophy has always appealed to me.

Sweating in a sweat lodge is an ancient Native American ritual, intended to purify the body and mind. The purpose of the exercise is to learn how to harness your thoughts. The extreme heat helps you excise pain, frustration, fear, and grief from your body and your mind. That is, if you are able to harness your thoughts.

The sweat lodge looks like a dome-shaped hut, a wigwam, and is comprised of branches covered with blankets. The leader throws water on a pile of red-hot, glowing stones stacked in the middle of the hut, which makes the inside extremely hot and smoky. The heat and smoke mimic the birth of the planet Earth.

I'd been curious about the sweat ceremony for some time, but in order to attend, you must be invited.

Last night, my friend Rob finally picked me up. We drove into Trancas Canyon, all the way up to the top of the mountain.

The Lakota/Sioux tribe owns the ground. They view the land as sacred. It has a beautiful view of Malibu and the South Bay.

Wolf, a Lakota/Sioux Indian, welcomed us. While waiting for the sun to set, he instructed us about the ceremony. Only during one of the four breaks were you allowed to leave and only after saying "For all our relations." There was no talking inside the tent.

The lodge was filling up with people. There was room for twenty, but we were fifty. It was packed. When it was dark out, someone closed the opening of the tent, and the ceremony began. We were seated on the cold earth in a circle around the hot stones. A Native American began to beat a drum and Wolf began his ritual singing in Lakota/Sioux. We repeated his words. I felt his pain and that of his ancestors. We chanted about gratitude for life and gratitude the beautiful things still to come our way. I started to get terribly hot and before long, I was soaked.

I could not stand it anymore. I had to get out. Don't panic, I said to myself. Harness your thoughts. It felt like an oven. My thoughts started to play tricks on me. At least you're not on the train to Auschwitz, I told myself. Gratitude? What for? Weren't they slaughtered, massacred?

Suddenly, I found myself in a packed cattle car ready to leave the station. Dogs barking, Nazis yelling, the locomotive whistled. I managed a spot near the door. On the platform, I saw a police officer arriving. With a loud bang, he closed the heavy cattle car door shut. There was no escaping.

We sat together on top of each other. Outside, someone wrote the number of passengers on the door. I was unable to harness my thoughts.

**

"Mother, have you ever wanted to take revenge?"

"What good does revenge do? Retaliation is counter productive. It'll consume you and hold you back from moving on. My father often said: A handshake takes more guts than turning your head away.

It's the handshake we need to accomplish.

*

Every night I feel so lucky to have a bed. I feel lucky to have sheets, blankets, indoor plumbing, and toilet tissue. My mom's story has made me grateful for all the things that seemed ordinary before.

**

"Mother, how did you walk through the mountains without shoes?"

"I do not remember anymore. There were very old shoes. I do not remember who gave them to me. I do not recall. For the life of me, I do not know anymore."

"You must have been scared."

"Herman and I were in the cattle car when they called our names and got us out. How could I have known that three days later, I would have been dead? That is impossible to imagine."

*

We were looking at a photo from before the war. She commented on her fingers. They weren't frostbitten yet.

A friend asked me why I'm always so grateful. I told him that I appreciated every moment that I'm not on the train to Auschwitz. Today, exactly so many years ago, was the day that my grand parents got off the train in Sobibor and walked right into the gas chamber.

I run on the beach. The feeling of freedom makes me feel giddy.

**

"Mother, did you ever see Malvine and her sister Mathilde again?"

"I wrote to them, but I got no reply. When I was in Israel in 1971, I asked around and found them. He had a shoe repair store. I went there and waited until she was done with a

customer. She turned to me and recognized me. We hugged and cried."

*

I enjoyed the time we spent together. We went to the village to eat a pancake. She eats very little these days. Nothing tastes good anymore. I ask her about the times she ate grass and potato peels.

**

"How was it, when you went home?"

"The return journey was difficult, because you feared for the future. If you went by the newspapers, we were so ungrateful. The only thing we thought of was money, they claimed. Today, when your house is robbed, the insurance pays. No insurance paid us. Even the monies that the German government paid to the Dutch government were not passed on to us."

*

She sits reading in her chair. I am lying on the couch. We swapped books. Now she's reading about Levison, who walked out of camp Westerbork, and I am reading *Night* by Elie Wiesel. We don't need to talk. We are both busy with the war. Her war. Day in, day out.

**

"Mother, did you think in 1943-1944 that only ten years later, you might be back with a new husband, four children, making dinner and doing laundry? How did you adjust? Was life normal again?"

"Never."

"Eight years later you had four children in school."

*

I am alone riding my bike. The path takes me over the beautiful dunes into a lush green wooded area with small lakes, drinking-water reservoirs for the western part of Holland. I see rabbits and deer, and listen to birds singing. I also see barbed wire, and a bunker. I get off my bike and climb up a lookout hill. I try to imagine what this place must've felt like during the war. It would've been illegal for me to even be there. I watched the lake. Its circumference seems similar to the shape of the map of Germany. In my imagination, the lake lifts itself upright. Blood starts flowing from the city of Berlin. The map of Germany fills with swastika flags. I hear footsteps of goose-step marching soldiers. I open my eyes. I sit on the bench on the hill. I hear the wind rushing past me. I feel my mother's pain. I continue my workout. How could a country be so beautiful with a history so horrid?

**

"Mother, do you still think of Herman?"
"Not knowing where he's buried was hard to accept. It's kept me wondering."

*

Her frost bitten fingers and toes saved her life. Had she been able to walk, her voice would have been silenced.

**

"It was hard to predict what was going to happen. We thought it was going to blow over. I felt safe, Herman told me we were going to be fine."

*

She looked fragile. We spent every moment together, except for that one-hour a day when I rode my bike, across the breathtaking dunes. From behind every tree, I saw an SS soldier jumping out at me. The dunes, the birds, the fresh air—what a beautiful countryside. There was no one in sight. The bicycle chain went click clack, click clack. The sound they must've heard inside the cattle car. I saw a rubber band on the bike path. I heard my mother's voice. Stop. Pick it up. In the camps, you would have bartered that for a piece of bread. Oh, Mother, please leave it, I insisted in vain.

"Mother, the dunes are so beautiful," I thankfully said, as I entered her apartment after my work out.

"Cup of tea?"

"Oh, good you're home. Help me with this will you."

I saw that she had confused the TV remote with the

120

phone.

I was packing to go back to the States. Her separation anxiety was working overtime.

**

"Mother, how do you feel about students reading your story?"

"They will be in charge one day and if they remember, maybe they can make peace for their children and grand-children, where previous generations have failed.

*

I'm running on Venice Beach and imagine signs posting "No Jews Allowed" on the boardwalk. Don't be stupid I told myself, that could never happen here. This is the United States.

Could it all happen again today? Let us never forget. Let us never surrender.

**

A generation of voices lost to the barbarity of history.
-Dr. Victoria Aarons, Professor and Chair, Department of English, Trinity University, San Antonio, Texas

Truth be told.
- Douglas L. Grice, Chief of Staff, Clinton Administration

An honorable contribution to Holocaust literature.
-Kirkus Discoveries

No matter how rough and tough Sonja's journey, the love in her survived and found a way to spring forward. Pelzman has done a great service reminding us of our humanity.
-Mary Lynn Navarro, Assistant Professor Kingsborough Community College, New York

An honest and compelling page-turner.
-Jack Ong, Executive Director Dr. Haing S. Ngor Foundation

A gripping read.
-Jack Polak, Chairman Emeritus of the Anne Frank Center USA and co-author of 'Steal a pencil for me.'

photo by Michael Faragher

Liliane Pelzman is a freelance writer and producer in Los Angeles.
